Future of Philanthropy

Insights from Multiple Expert Discussions Around the World

Contents

1. Foreword from our Global Patron — 4
2. Thanks to our Global Patron and Regional Hosts — 6
3. Introduction — 8
4. Executive Summary — 10
5. Top 15 Shifts Identified by Global Workshops — 12
6. Context — 18
7. Thematic Drivers of Future Change — 20
8. The Changing Ways to Give — 47
9. Concluding Thoughts — 52
10. Questions for the Future — 53

Appendices

1. Key Insights from Global Workshops — 54

Foreword from our Global Patron Badr Jafar

No one can predict the future, yet we can strive to become better informed about what is ahead and use that information to be better change makers, enablers and impact-driven almsgivers. It is with this spirit that I have engaged with and supported this global Future Agenda programme on the Future of Philanthropy. The programme seeks to embrace the convergence of seemingly disconnected experiences worldwide in order to share a unified perspective of the forces shaping philanthropy over the next decade. The hope is that doing so will help enhance these diverse philanthropic efforts' impact going forward.

Philanthropy, or private resources for the public good, has a huge positive benefit on society and the world in which we live. Our individual and collective desire to maximise positive impact means that as the world continues to evolve, so too must the practice of philanthropy. This report demonstrates that shifts in Power, Knowledge and Trust will provide both opportunity and challenge for those who wish to make the biggest difference most effectively. It also identifies many drivers and insights that will shape this landscape over next decade.

By way of example, I'd like to pull out four expected trends that stood out for me:

1) The next wave of globalisation will lead to a major increase in private philanthropic investment. Economic power will also continue to move southward and eastward. The fastest evolving markets, including the Middle East, Africa, Developing Asia, India, China and Latin America, will increasingly fortify and sustain themselves with less or little dependence on so-called 'western markets'. If properly cultivated, we should expect a similar shift in philanthropy, and the resultant lasting social change that will take place in these global growth markets.

2) At the same time, a new millennial philanthropic generation is rapidly emerging, inheriting not only massive wealth but also holding different beliefs and assumptions from their predecessors about how to optimise impact. To put this into context, it is projected that in the coming 10 years, 14,000 ultra-high net worth individuals globally are expected to pass on USD 3.9 trillion to the next generation, with a further USD 26 trillion passed on within the subsequent 20 years. The huge pool of philanthropic capital that will emanate from these inheritors can and should go a long way in addressing some of the acute social and environmental challenges they will also inherit.

3) Although statistics indicate that faith-based giving has witnessed a steady decline in the US, in other parts of the world this form of giving is on the rise and has been recognized as a vastly underutilised resource for achieving the Sustainable Development Goals (SDGs). For example, with Islamic philanthropy even a small fraction of current Zakat and Sadaqah – compulsory and discretionary almsgiving by Muslim donors which is estimated at between USD 250 billion to USD 1 trillion annually – applied in a coordinated manner could significantly contribute to global development and humanitarian aid requirements.

4) Another area offering huge potential is the increased availability of and desire for transparent information and the resulting insights generated through the application of data analytics. While data in and of itself is no panacea, there is no doubt that it will increasingly be used to make informed policy and philanthropic decisions. This is exciting, as it is clear that those who seek to maximize the impact of philanthropy and social investing today are keen on changing the current state of paucity of data, transparency and effective feedback loops, which if optimised would ultimately result in enhanced levels of trust between all stakeholders in the philanthropy nexus.

With rising global need, we simply must do better than the status quo. My hope is that this style of open collaboration helps all to make progress more quickly and more effectively. Sincere thanks go to all who have contributed to and enabled this programme and the valuable insights generated. We look forward to continuing this important dialogue and to building a more equitable world together.

Badr Jafar

Thanks to our Regional Hosts

The Future of Philanthropy Programme was organised in partnership with a number of leading organisations around the world. We would like to acknowledge and thank them for their collaboration and support. In particular we would like to thank our Global Patron Badr Jafar for his continued support of the initiative. This global foresight programme was made possible by their generosity and that of the participants who chose to join the workshops. The enthusiasm of all those attending our events shows that there is an appetite to share experiences, explore ideas, consider options and identify future directions. We thank them, most sincerely.

We would also like to thank Professor Cathy Pharoah, Visiting Professor of Charity Funding and Co-Director of the Centre for Charitable Giving and Philanthropy at Cass Business School.

In addition, we would also like to thank The Pearl Initiative and Philanthropy Age in encouraging the production and sharing of this report.

Washington DC
GlobalGiving
FEEDBACK LABS

Quito
asobanca
CONSEJO METROPOLITANO DE RESPONSABILIDAD SOCIAL

Dubai
مبادرات محمد بن راشد آل مكتوم العالمية
Mohammed Bin Rashid
Al Maktoum Global Initiatives

London
THE FORE

NPC
New Philanthropy Capital

Kuala Lumpur
ALPHA CATALYST CONSULTING

Mumbai
ankur capital

ROADS AHEAD CONSULTING
THE FUTURE OF GROWTH

Oxford
SAID BUSINESS SCHOOL
SKOLL CENTRE FOR SOCIAL ENTREPRENEURSHIP
UNIVERSITY OF OXFORD

Singapore
LIEN Centre for Social Innovation
SINGAPORE MANAGEMENT UNIVERSITY

avpn
Asian Venture Philanthropy Network

London
BRITISH ASIAN TRUST
TRANSFORMING LIVES TOGETHER

Introduction

This report is written for anyone with an interest in philanthropy and how to make it more effective with higher impact in the future. We hope it will be useful to individuals, charities and other NGO's, businesses and governments as well as advisors to each of these audiences.

Taking the long view has never been easy. However, as change accelerates in an increasingly connected world, more organisations are looking further ahead to better understand emerging opportunities and threats. We believe that sharing knowledge across disciplines and across continents can add real value to the process, particularly as often innovation occurs at the intersection of different industries disciplines and challenges.

There are a host of changes that we need to think about when considering the next ten years. Some are incremental evolutions, and some are radical revolutions. The big challenge in any foresight programme is in differentiating these and gaining a clear understanding of which changes are most likely

The intention of this report is to consolidate expert views from nine workshops in seven countries around the future of philanthropy and how it will develop. This understanding will make it easier to shape a strategy that will address upcoming challenges and opportunities. We offer a summary of the key trends and drivers that will be influential and identify areas of potential change. As such the report provides insight about the leading edge of philanthropy today as well as where it might go in the future.

Our hope is that this will enable you to make a bigger difference for society in the years to come.

futureagenda

Launched in 2010, the Future Agenda programme is the world's largest global open foresight initiative. Taking place every five years, its aim is to identify and better understand societal issues in a global context.

The intention of the Future Agenda process is not only to obtain new views around the multiple topics explored but also to understand perspectives about the directions we should take, why, and with what consequence. To do this, recognised experts from a wide range of disciplines, are invited to answer a number of common questions on the future. These are published as initial perspectives and become the basis for ongoing, facilitated debate. In 2015 initial perspectives were developed across 24 different subjects that address everything from the future of health, energy, cities and work to the future of data, privacy and money. A minimum of 4 workshops on each topic were held across multiple geographies in order to identify the big issues, emerging challenges and cultural complexities for the next decade. In total over 120 workshops were held in 35 countries and as a result, well informed people from many different cultures, of different ages and with multiple perspectives, were able to contribute in person. Many thousands more participated online.

Between the major 5-year global programmes, each year we explore other topics of interest in more detail. In 2016, alongside bespoke research undertaken for a number of organisations, Future Agenda ran the Future of Cities project. This was another major open foresight study involving workshops in 12 locations engaging with leading thinkers. The summary output of this project is available on slide-share and as a new report. Since then, other topics have included the Future of Surgery and the Future of Automotive Data.

The core insights for the entire programme are shared via multiple platforms so that we can all be more informed on what others think about the next decade and so make better decisions. As well as online materials on slideshare and flickr, in 2016 two books have been published – 'The World in 2025' and 'Six Challenges for the Next Decade'.

For 2018, the first key focus area has been in investigating the Future of Philanthropy – a global exploration of emerging changes at the intersection of philanthropy and impact investing.

Methodology

The Future of Philanthropy research began in 2017 when we Team invited Professor Cathy Pharaoh, Co-Director of the Centre for Charitable Giving at Cass Business School to write an initial perspective. This gave an overview of the current status of the sector, identified challenges and opportunities ahead and suggested ways forward. The team then used this to stimulate further debate in nine high level discussions which were held in Dubai, Kuala Lumpur, London (x2), Mumbai, Oxford, Quito, Singapore and Washington DC. Each conversation built on the ideas expressed and insights developed from preceding workshops.

In all, more than 200 experts drawn from academia, business, government, advisory, charities and non-governmental organisations (NGOs) gave their time and energy to join a workshop. In addition, many others commented, either online or in interviews. The Future Agenda then synthesised the output and supported the insights with case studies and examples.

This report provides an overview of the collective debate and, where useful, includes references to other areas of research.

Executive Summary

This decade sees philanthropy at a pivotal point. The evolving geopolitical landscape, the rapid creation of new wealth and a greater awareness of how philanthropy can create social change have already led to exciting innovation and new thinking. This is influencing approaches to giving and social responsibility across the world.

During our conversations three interconnected drivers of change were identified. They are Power, Knowledge and, inherent to both of these, Trust. They will shape the evolution of philanthropy over the next decade.

During our conversations three interconnected drivers of change were identified. They are Power, Knowledge and, inherent to both of these, Trust

Theme 1: Power. Exerting power and influence to create positive change has always been a key element of philanthropy. Looking ahead the experts we spoke to expect increasing fluidity over who holds power and how it is exerted, managed and regulated. As the centre of wealth shifts east and southwards a new global elite will emerge with greater female representation, and a technological mindset. This new generation, brought up at the cusp of the century will challenge traditional orthodoxies. Similarly, corporate interest and participation in building shared value for a wider set of stakeholders will ensure that the lines between "who does good" and "who drives profit" will become increasingly blurred.

In this time of fluidity, the role of the state to provide both leadership and deliver effective regulation will be critical. In particular a key challenge will be how to best unleash local, community-based philanthropy and sustain and grow smaller and medium sized delivery organisations.

Theme 2: Knowledge.

Greater knowledge and understanding, together with working feedback loops, were viewed as essential pre-cursors to more impactful philanthropy. However, while an increase in more data driven philanthropy is widely expected to deliver improvement across the board, basic human nature will ensure that emotional giving continues to mitigate the ultra-rationalist promise of effective altruism.

Greater knowledge is also expected to lead to an increase in the development of collaborative solutions and an appreciation of the need to invest in philanthropic capacity. It is also expected that on-going efforts to share knowledge for the benefit of all as well as harness new media to spread it more effectively, will further grow philanthropic impact.

Theme 3: Trust:

There has always been a degree of both private and public scepticism around philanthropy and philanthropists, and, as in other walks of life, this distrust has been growing in the last decade. While cause and effect is impossible to prove, it is interesting that this has occurred at the same time as the gap between the rich and the poor has increased. Perhaps this is because wealth is increasingly concentrated in the hands of the few. Indeed some in our workshops referred to the emergence of a global philanthropic oligarchy.

In order to achieve their goals, change-making philanthropists, at any scale, must seek to build and maintain trust in the communities in which they operate. In the next decade, workshop participants identified the need to address three elements in order to achieve this:

- The need to behave with integrity, acting transparently and democratically;
- The need to be reliable, acting consistently – even when times are tough; and
- Competence, the ability to deliver results.

In terms of creating more philanthropic impact, two cross-cutting ideas surfaced repeatedly:

- Digital technology – This was viewed as the critical underpinning that will provide more effective mechanisms to give, deliver more impact and do this in a way that enables deeper learning, engagement and transparency.
- Long-term collaborations – There is a shift from short-term approaches towards increased support for longer-term, collaborative solutions that seek to address the root causes of a social or environmental challenge in a holistic way. For many this reflects a general shift in attitude as the millennial generation gains influence. Notably both ideas are equally applicable to philanthropy at all scales, from community based social entrepreneurs to global collaborations

Schumpeter's waves of creative destruction, powered by the digital technologies that define our era, are expected to ensure that over the next decade changes will accelerate. As societal attitudes, behaviours and commercial common sense adjust to a connected and data driven digital world, so too will philanthropy.

Top 15 shifts

At each of the workshops, experts were asked to rank a series of insights. They used their judgement to assess relevance to the topic of philanthropy in the next decade.

Top 15 Future Shifts (Global Average)

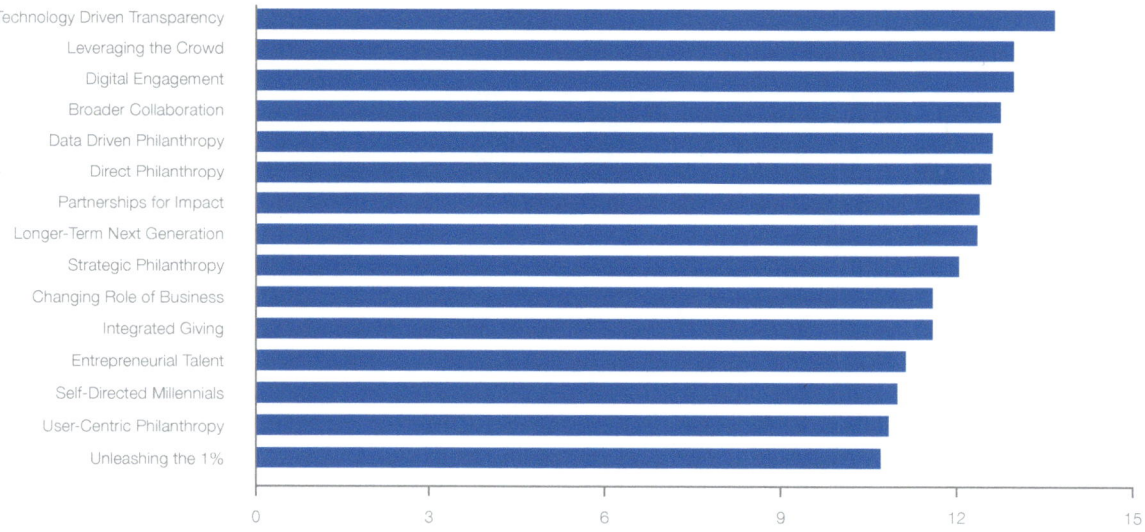

Each workshop, typically comprised 25-30 diverse experts drawn from Government, NGO, academia, business, advisory etc. The experts were split into 5 groups and each group was given a set of c.25 insight cards to discuss and sort into three piles. Experts were asked to sort (High, Medium, Low) by relevance, importance and impact for the next decade. The insights were then scored High (3 points), Medium (2 points) and Low (1 point) and the results for each insight across all groups were calculated. A top score of 15 would indicate that all tables ranked the insight as highly relevant, important and impactful and is indicated along the X axis of the above chart.

The insights can be seen in full here:

https://www.slideshare.net/futureagenda2/future-of-high-impact-philanthropy-updated-view

Top 15 Future Shifts (Dubai Average)

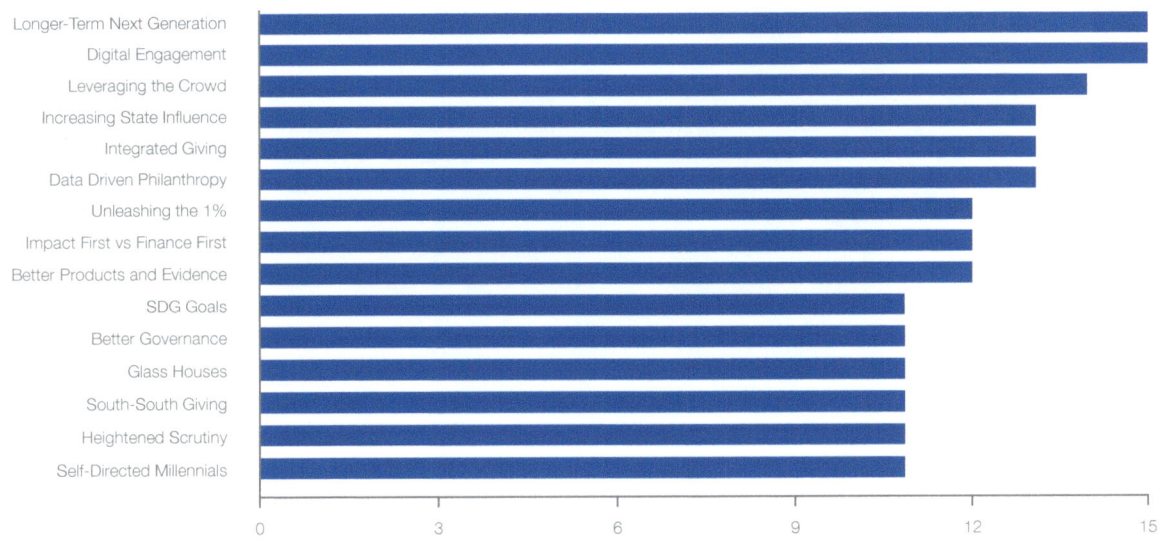

Top 15 Future Shifts (Mumbai Average)

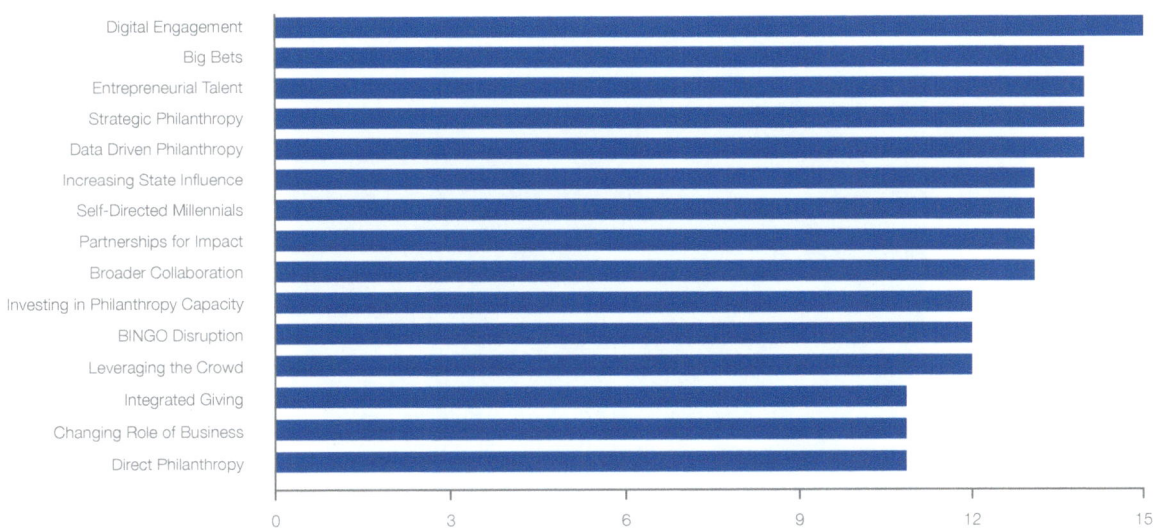

Top 15 Future Shifts (Singapore Average)

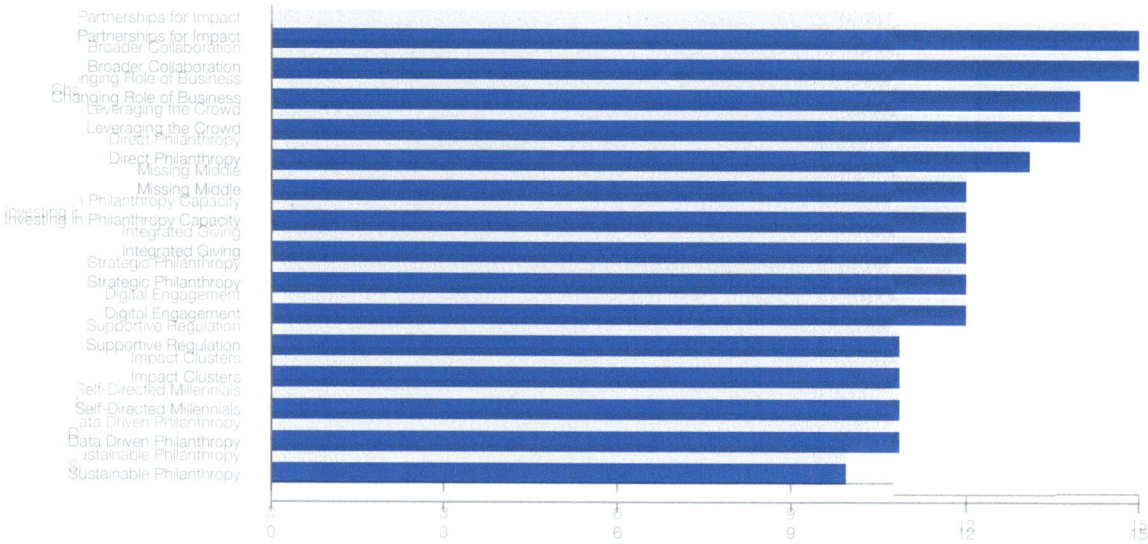

Top 15 Future Shifts (Kuala Lumpur Average)

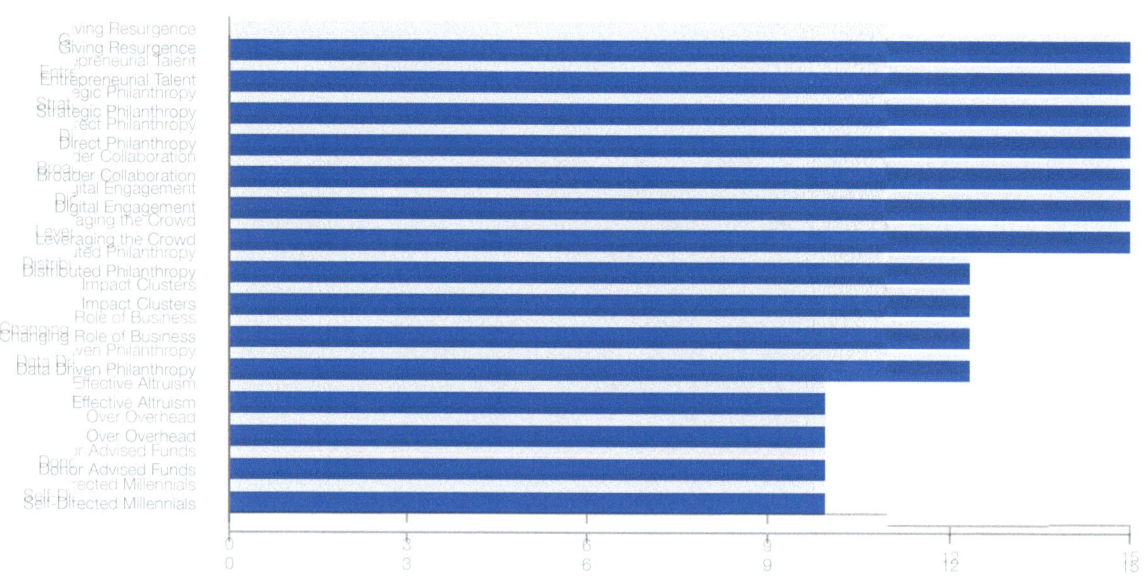

Top 15 Future Shifts (Oxford Average)

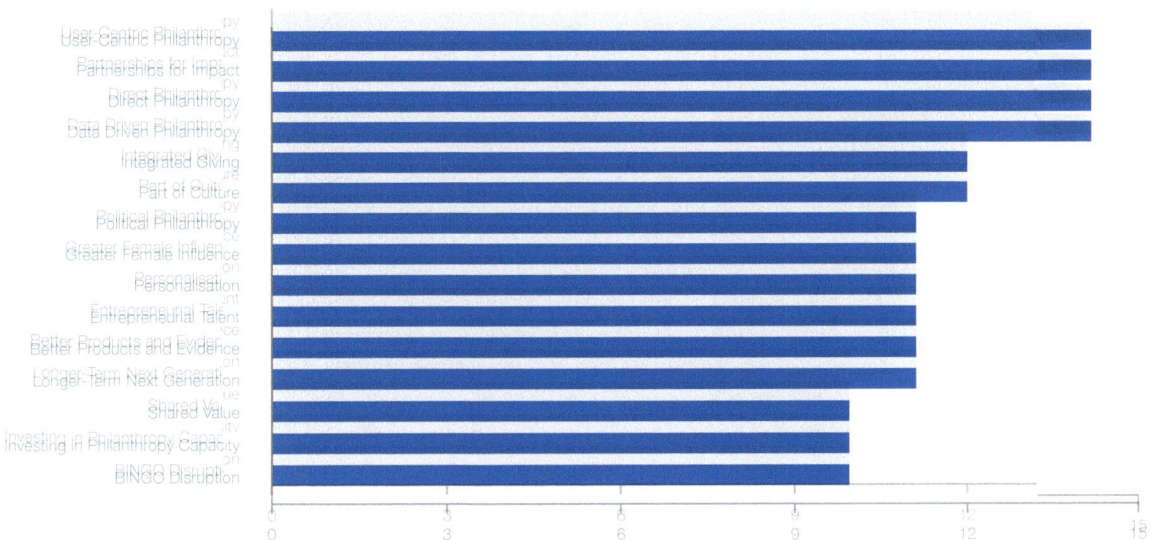

Top 15 Future Shifts (London Average)

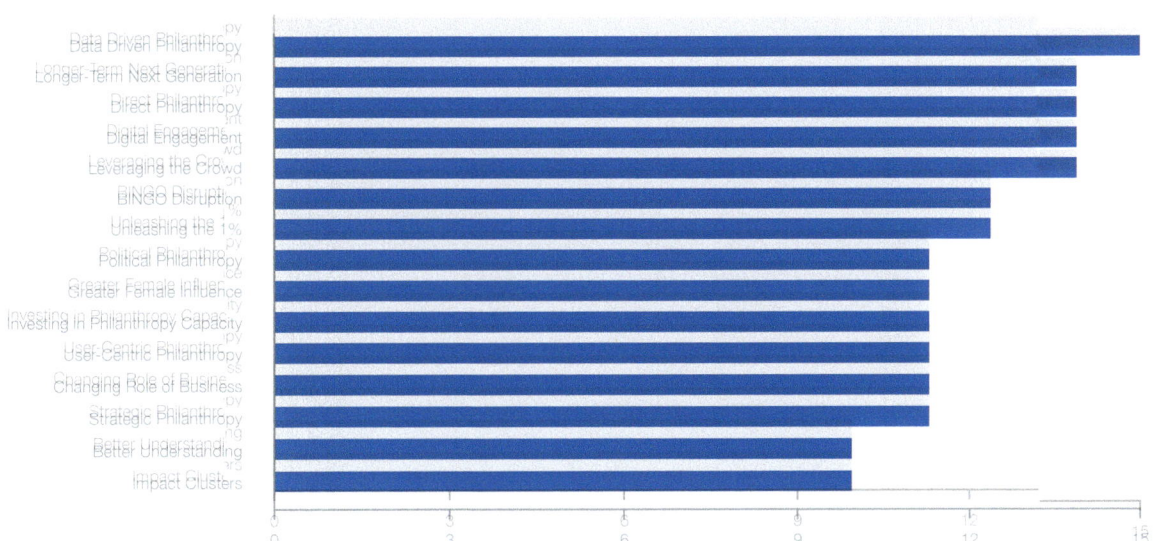

Top 15 Future Shifts (British Asian Trust Average)

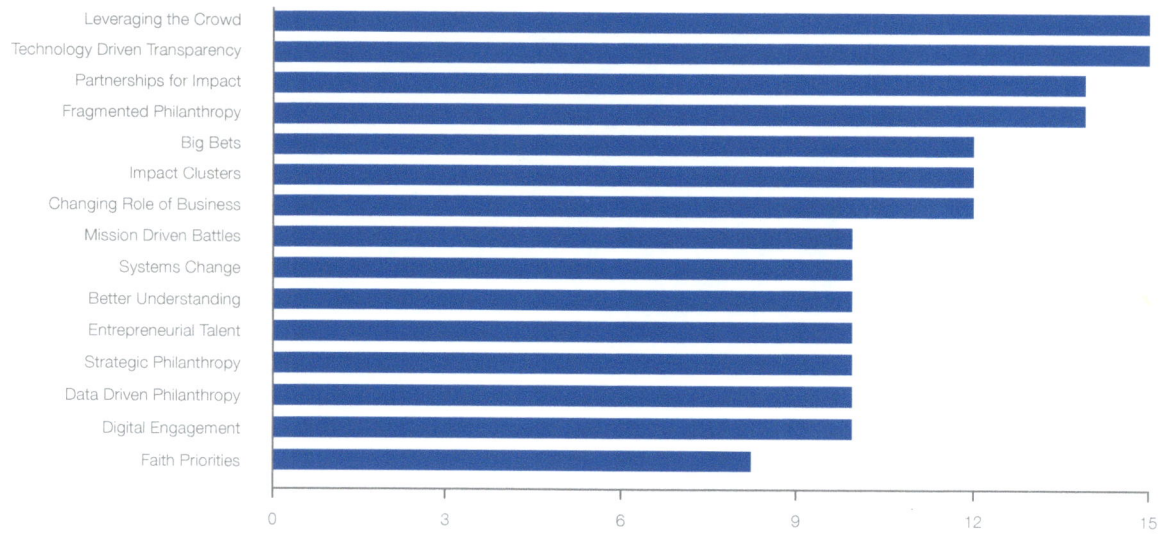

Top 15 Future Shifts (Washington Average)

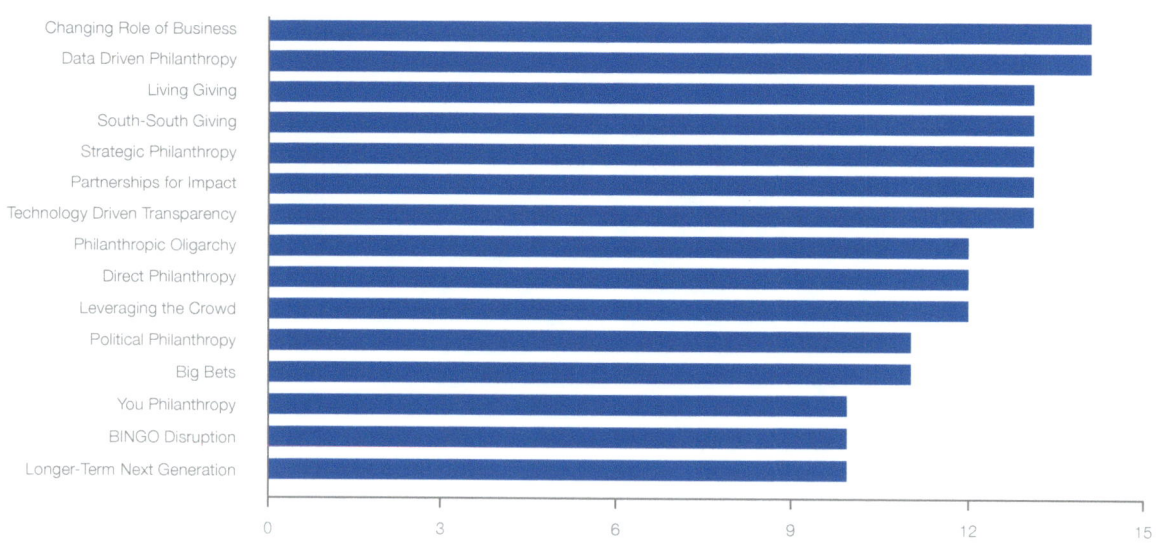

Top 15 Future Shifts (Quito Average)

Partnerships for Impact	13
Digital Engagement	13
Technology Driven Transparency	13
Increasing State Influence	12
Political Philanthropy	12
Power Shifts	12
User-Centric Philanthropy	12
Longer-Term Next Generation	12
You Philanthropy	11
Greater Female Influence	11
Changing Role of Business	11
Direct Philanthropy	11
Leveraging the Crowd	11
Data Driven Philanthropy	10
Who does good (blurred lines)	9

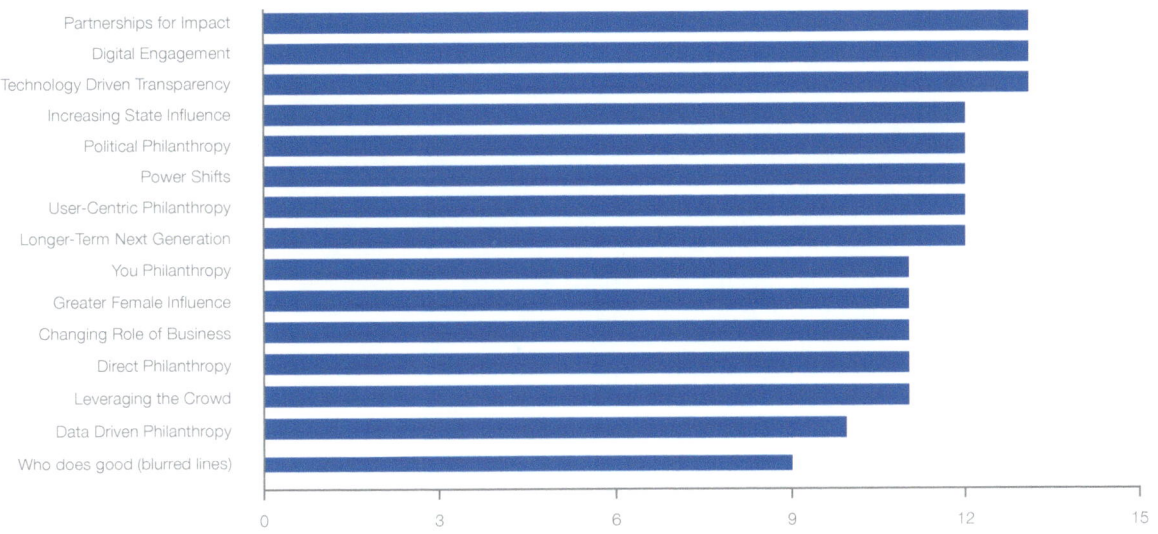

Context

The Past

Charitable giving has been embedded in most religions, societies and cultures for millennia. It has taken different forms and purposes, many of which are still reflected today.

For many the Scottish-American industrialist Andrew Carnegie (1835-1919), the richest man of his time, set the standard for modern giving. During the last 18 years of his life he gave around 90 percent of his fortune to charities, foundations, and universities, a sum equivalent to about $78.6 billion in 2017. He also galvanised others to do the same; in 1889 he wrote an article, "The Gospel of Wealth", which inspired an unprecedented wave of philanthropy amongst his peers. Carnegie was by no means alone for his time: Other industrialists such as India's Jamsetji Tata bequeathed much of their personal wealth for the benefit of others as did Henry Ford in the US. At a time when government funding was not available the main requirements were often to provide housing, healthcare and education.

Today

We have had a century of progress since then and yet the need for philanthropy remains just as great. Some argue that we are living in an increasingly fractious and difficult time. The issues that we face such as climate change, loss of biodiversity, water shortages, global pandemics, the mass movement of peoples; the endless destruction wrought by war not to mention the constant need to address social inequality, grinding poverty and disease seem to be growing exponentially, despite the valiant efforts of some to, at least, contain them. The complexity of many of these issues extend beyond national boundaries and affect the wealthy as well as the poor. Coincidentally for some nations, economic downturn has seen a reduction or closure of public services. All this when public trust in the long-established institutions of religion, business, government, NGOs, and the media is in long-term broad decline.

Keeping the faith: Despite considerable changes in attitudes to philanthropy, faith-based donations are a major focus for much of the world. In the Middle East a recent survey suggested that around two-thirds of all giving is motivated by religion.[i] In the Netherlands it is 40 per cent and the US 32 per cent.[ii] Indeed one of the reasons why Myanmar tops the 2017 CAF World Giving Index, an authoritative annual data driven review of how and why people give in 139 countries, may well be because the widespread practice of Theravada Buddhism encourages it. The challenge for the future is that increasing secularism in some countries alongside growing public distrust of different religious organisations means that it is increasingly difficult for some faith-based charities to remain effective. There are fears, particularly in the West, that in the future this prejudice may prevent them from playing a bigger societal role. This is certainly the case in the US where religious giving has experienced a steady decline, accounting for 50 per cent of donations in 1990 to 32 percent in 2016.[iii]

It is certainly true that there are challenges but at the same time there is opportunity and optimism. Many philanthropists, large and small are prepared to put their energy into finding better solutions than we have at the moment.

The result of this is huge variation, and sometimes contradiction in how problems are addressed: The super-wealthy individual donor versus crowd-based approaches; the targeting of major world issues, such those identified in the United Nation's Sustainable Development Goals, at the same time as a move towards local activism and support of overstretched public services; a focus on speed of delivery at the same time as the acknowledgement that complex social issues require time and consideration, not to mention the need for reliable investment in research and development; the demand for transparency and collaboration at the same time as a growing appetite for independent action continues to grow. "Doing Good Well" it seems has never been more difficult. Equally there have never been so many people, in so many different ways, prepared to give it a go.

Thematic Drivers of Future Change

What is clear from all our discussions is that we are seeing a fundamental shift in when we give, how we give, how we receive and how change is created through philanthropy. Although some points discussed during the workshops were specific to individual locations, across our discussions we found three thematic drivers of change: Power, Knowledge and, inherent to both of these, Trust.

Theme 1: Power

Exerting power and influence to create positive change has always been a key element of philanthropy. As we move into the fourth industrial revolution, defined by globalisation and digital technologies, we are witnessing increasing fluidity over who holds power and influence and how it is exerted. Philanthropy, particularly how it is managed and regulated, is part of that power mix.

The Role of the State

Broadly speaking state involvement in philanthropic initiatives was viewed in two ways in our workshops. In Dubai, for example, it was seen as helpful, providing leadership, clarity of direction and a beacon for collaboration. However, others felt government interventions were too controlling and constraining, prioritising some issues and dismissing others and often suppressing the wishes of civil society.

Political upheaval and economic insecurity has seen many governments in the West reduce and redirect their spending on both public services and foreign aid. In some cases, charities and private donors are plugging the gaps with the provision of food banks, health care and even housing. The US National Council on Non-Profits believes that the 2018 State of the Sector Survey produced by the Nonprofit Financial Fund will show that there has now been an increasing gap between state provision and the needs of communities for a decade. The Red Cross is among a number of organisations that have been running food banks both in the UK and the USA– despite being two of the richest countries in the world, dramatic policy changes have resulted in an increase in the number of people in need of help.

Some in our workshops believe that elected representatives should take a more interventionist approach to this. They argue that those accountable under the democratic system should safeguard key services for the vulnerable such as health and medicine, rather than shift the burden on to independent, unaccountable organisations – however well-meaning – to prop them up. Others also pointed out that it would be unwise for governments to become over reliant on continuous support from the third sector. Some charities also resent what they see as the need to make up for government failure to address its most basic of responsibilities. Bill Gates, among others, has already warned that organisations like his are "absolutely not" prepared to fill the holes in public spending that are the result of changes in government policy.[iv]

Globally governments are taking increasingly innovative approaches to plugging the funding gap. Introduced in 2014, India's 2% Corporate Social Responsibility (CSR) tax is often cited as one of the world's most interesting experiments to promote private philanthropy. This has made it mandatory for corporations with revenues of more than 10 billion rupees (approximately $131 million) to give two percent of their profits to charities. Essentially the objective is to push India's corporate sector to provide the seed capital and philanthropy to find solutions to India's most challenging problems in areas such as education, healthcare, the environment and skills development. However, while hailed as ground-breaking in intent, many have been critical of its implementation. Australia's Deakin University reported, "Our analysis shows that the law in its current form is failing to promote CSR activity. Its poor design and lack of clear obligations, set in a milieu of poor law enforcement, is also not generating an ethical obligation to obey the law in spirit."

Whatever you think of its effectiveness, and many would agree it is cumbersome, this initiative sets precedent which others might well follow. A number of governments are studying its success and failure and, looking ahead, a more refined version may well emerge – either as an evolution in India itself or as a new initiative in another quarter.

Another example of State influence is the UAE's 2017 The Year of Giving. In its own words, "The UAE National Strategy for the Year of Giving is a comprehensive plan to institutionalise humanitarianism in the public and private sectors. It stems from a vision to consolidate humanitarian work and establish the UAE as the most philanthropic country in the world." Initiated by the President, His Highness Sheikh Khalifa bin Zayed Al Nahyan, and supported by the UAE Vice President and Prime Minister and Ruler of Dubai, His Highness Sheikh Mohamed bin Rashid Al Maktoum, the 2017 Year of Giving policies provided a comprehensive framework for philanthropy through initiatives, strategies and programmes intended to celebrate the virtues of giving and cement philanthropy into the heart of the nation. There are, however, other views of this. In several of our workshops the approved UAE shortlist for giving was highlighted as an example of excessive state influence. As one participant pointed out, "If your charity is not on the shortlist then either you are forbidden from giving, or if you do give, via, for example, the Red Crescent, then there is a 30% to 50% handling fee for the transaction."

Not all governments have been keen to stimulate private and corporate philanthropy. The Hudson Institute's Index of Philanthropic Freedom provides a fascinating insight into philanthropic freedom across the world. By examining barriers and incentives for individuals and organizations to donate money and time to social causes, the Institute's Center for Global Prosperity measured, ranked, and compared 64 countries on their ease of giving and identified a number of themes which have shaped philanthropic freedom. These include; the unintended consequence of foreign exchange regulations, IFF legislation and more deliberate attempts to legislate against foreign intervention – as illustrated by Russia's foreign agent law.

Sometimes legacy regulation makes it difficult even for local donors. While certainly not the worst in the world, giving to causes of their choice has been a challenge historically for Chinese philanthropists. This may explain why the China Philanthropy

Research Institute estimates that 80% of the top 100 philanthropists from mainland China's donations go to overseas charities. Many may well have preferred to give to local causes, but hitherto regulations have hindered the development of philanthropy at home. In addition, other than a generous spirit there were not many incentives to give, so until recently not-for-profit organisations had few if any tax benefits and were obliged to have a government partner, which inevitably curbed autonomy. Today, things are beginning to change. The government is now more open to the benefits of philanthropic support from business and individuals and China's first-ever Charity Law, was put in place in 2016, to ease restrictions on fundraising and operational activities of charity groups. Also in 2016, the Ministry of Civil affairs approved 13 charitable organisations online philanthropy forms. Among these was Tencent Philanthropy, now well-known as part of the online platform Tencent's 9/9 Day of giving. This has gained widespread public support. The 2017 Day of Giving, which actually takes place over 3 days, generated of 1.3Bn RMB of donations of which came from public donations, 23% from the Tencent Foundation and 14% from social enterprise. Overall almost 13m donors made contributions to over 6,400 charitable projects.[vi] These changes may herald an increased mainstreaming of philanthropy in China.

A final note. Some participants also observed the increasing difficulty of moving philanthropic funds across borders (e.g. in Egypt and Pakistan) as a result of increased Government legislation. Often philanthropy is inadvertently being unnecessarily embroiled in wider anti-money laundering (AML) or finance of terrorism (CFT) rules. Whatever the cause, finding ways to increase the global liquidity of legitimate philanthropic flows can only be a good thing.

Corporate Philanthropy Blurring the Lines

Corporates are not only giving more but they are also increasingly doing it in different ways, blurring the lines between "who does good" and "who drives profit". According to data from Philanthropy outlook, corporate giving in the US has grown at 1.6x the rate of individual giving over the last 40 years, with average

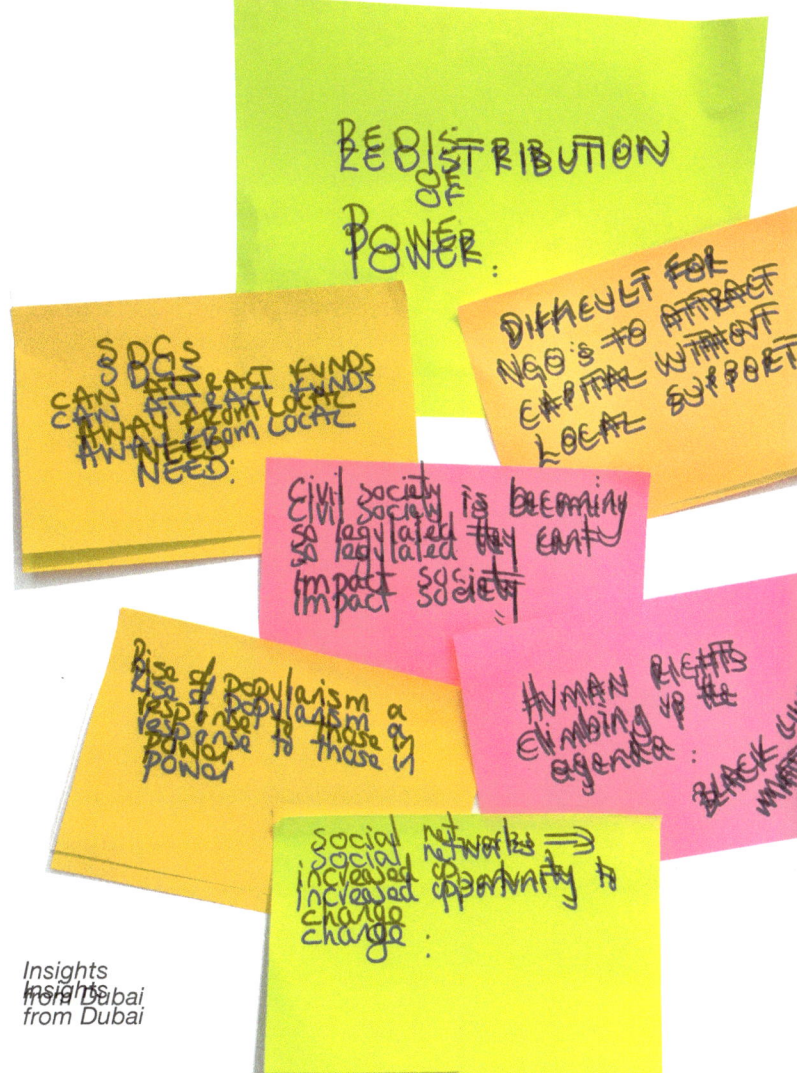

Insights from Dubai

annual growth running at 5.9 per cent. Clearly, despite the oft-quoted argument made by Milton Friedman in a 1970 New York Times Magazine article, that the, "... one social responsibility of business... [is] to increase its profits," more and more corporates are involved in philanthropy. Usually, the type of giving involved consists of numerous small cash donations to aid local causes or the provision of operating support to well-established national charities, made in the belief that this generates goodwill among employees, customers, and the local community. Beyond this, some enlightened businesses are extending their definition of what doing good means to find opportunities to help to address society's problems. Reflecting Porter & Kramer's concept of shared value, some are aligning their philanthropy with issues close to their brand, for example Barclays in financial education, the outdoor apparel retailer Patagonia on environmental causes and the like. Looking ahead and from a sector standpoint, many in our workshops believe that companies will make the most impact by focusing their donations on initiatives which address the social topics aligned with their current way of doing business, for example carbon (transport and housing), inequality (finance), diabetes and obesity (food), human and workers' rights (retail).

It's perfectly easy to see that this new burst of interest in corporate responsibility is self-serving, providing useful PR opportunities and increasing employee satisfaction levels at comparatively low cost. But it is also effective. Companies often have unique capabilities – distribution fleets, huge social media audiences, not to mention public trust in their ability to actually meet targets in a timely and cost-efficient manner. All this puts them on the front foot when they begin to build philanthropy into their underlying business model. And the interest runs both ways; galvanised by the Sustainable Development Goals and the realisation that meeting them requires harnessing

> The lines between purely for-profit and purely non-profit efforts, or "who does good" and "who drives profit", are blurring, many believe with wider beneficial impact.

private capital and creating durable private sector solutions, increased collaboration with business is seen as a key imperative both for government and philanthropic donors going forward. On top of this, businesses are well positioned to act as social change incubators through non-profit partnerships, can offer prize philanthropy and, with greater focus, deliver socially conscious business models.

One impact of this of this increased cross-sector collaboration is that the lines between purely for-profit and purely non-profit efforts, or "who does good" and "who drives profit", are blurring,

Corporate Social Responsibility and Corporate Shared Value, Porter & Kramer

CSR → CSV

CSR
- Values: doing good
- Citizenship, philanthropy, sustainability
- Discretionary or in response to external pressure
- Seperate from profit maximization
- Agenda is determined by external reporting and personal preferences
- impact limited by corporate footprint and CSR budget

Example: Fair trade purchasing

CSV
- Values: economic and societal benefite relative to cost
- joint company and community value creation
- Integral to competing
- Integral to profit maximization
- Agenda is company specific and internally generated
- Realigns the entire company budget

Example: Transforming procurement to increase quality and yield

[Source: https://hbr.org/2011/01/the-big-idea-creating-shared-value]

many believe with wider beneficial impact. Driven by top-down support from company boardrooms such as Unilever, Patagonia and Tata, alongside bottom-up employee momentum, philanthropy through initiatives such as matched funding and community events, is becoming an integral part of broader social change, whether it be delivering new programmes such as the collaboration between Mastercard and DataKind or supporting existing models such as Johnson & Johnson's 30-year collaboration with Save the Children. Clearly Social Return on Investment (SROI) is now a core part of more agendas and many see that it has an increasing role in reshaping the economy. A few in our workshops foresee that in order to drive broader social change, more companies will appoint, as Salesforce.com has a Chief Philanthropy Officer who both ensures sustained contributions and coordinates activities across foundations, pledges, industry initiatives and employee-driven actions.

There is always a "but" however. A trusted brand remains essential. Some industries have been permanently damaged by past behaviours: There is widespread concern about pharmaceutical support for academic research despite the obvious advantages of drug development mechanisms and commercial expertise pharmaceuticals companies can bring to such collaborations; an oil company may well want to support the arts or improve the living conditions for vulnerable communities, but such is the sector's poor reputation it may be difficult for the recipient to accept. Even household brands can fall foul of public distrust.

Walmart gives away over $1bn in cash and product annually – but it's still viewed as one of the world's least responsible companies, and is a continual target of boycotts and protests.

> FOCUS ON TRUST
>
> NON PROFIT PARTNERSHIPS DRIVE POSITIVE CHANGE
>
> PRIVATE PHILANTHROPY HAS LESS CHECKS + BALANCES → BUT GROWING :)
>
> BALANCE PROFIT WITH RESPONSIBILITY
>
> The challenge to philanthropy by populist backlash will cause a debate on corporate + income tax systems. It may also deter or shift personal philanthropy
>
> BLURRED LINE BETWEEN CHARITY + BUSINESS → SOCIALLY MINDED BUSINESS.
>
> Business as social change incubators.

Insights from Oxford

That said, some brands have been able to make a huge contribution to society at the same time as running a highly profitable commercial operation. Take Unilever whose foundation is, "dedicated to improving the quality of life through the provision of hygiene, sanitation, access to clean drinking water, basic nutrition, and enhancing self-esteem". The company works with and funds initiatives alongside organisations such as Oxfam and the World Food Program. Given that a large proportion of its business is in the provision of personal care such as soaps and toothpaste, and home care such as water purifiers and toilet cleaning products, supporting these causes it is a case of business objectives marrying well with added public good.

And yet the road is not always a smooth one, even for the likes of Unilever. Consider for example the conundrum if, as happened in Cambodia, the best sanitation solution for a rural community is to have dry toilets that do not need Unilever's products to keep them clean.

Looking forward, as the balance of power shifts away from corporate philanthropy into the hands of private individuals, the frequency of dilemmas such as these may decline – but so too may the transparency around money flows and the accountability of donors. Certainly, the line between private and corporate philanthropy is becoming increasingly blurred.

The Global Elite - changing philanthropic flows

According to The Guardian, commenting on the latest UBS / PWC "Billionaires Report", "the world's super-rich hold the greatest concentration of wealth since the US Gilded Age at the turn of the 20th century when families like the Carnegies, Rockefellers and Vanderbilts controlled vast fortunes."[viii] Today the global elite are an international crew. And, as the centre of economic power shifts eastwards, Asian billionaires are beginning to outnumber their American counterparts and are expected to overtake them in financial clout by 2021.

From a philanthropic perspective, the good news is that increasingly, high net worth individuals (HNWIs) are prepared to donate both time and money to good causes. Melissa Berman, president of Rockefeller Philanthropy Advisors, a non-profit philanthropic advisory firm puts it, "wealthy people who are getting engaged in philanthropy also want to be knowledgeable about the issues that they care about. They really want to take a deep dive and spend their time and their energy, as well as their money."[ix] This is particularly noticeable in the US where a flurry of billionaires have committed extraordinary resources to solving global issues.

However, some are sceptical of this largesse – particularly in light of the highly publicized tax controversies that have plagued the tech sector. Although there are extremely attractive tax incentives that encourage philanthropic giving, particularly in the US, it is worth remembering that rich people don't need to donate money; generally they can protect themselves from the world's worst outcomes and many do just that.

Those who choose to give, do so significantly. The Gates Foundation has donated $28 billion; Warren Buffett has contributed similarly; and the Chan Zuckerberg Initiative has earmarked US$3 billion to "cure, prevent or manage all disease".

Billionaires are also encouraging other billionaires to "do the decent thing". The Giving Pledge, founded by Warren Buffett and Bill and Melinda Gates, is this century's version of "The Gospel of Wealth". Established in 2010, it asks the world's richest individuals to commit to give away more than half of it away.

Large scale giving is increasingly a global phenomenon. Overall the Wealth X 2017 report suggests that, it continues to grow at the predicted rate, an additional US$260bn could be in play for philanthropic causes in the coming years. It seems the rate of giving is also increasing – there has been a sharp rise since 2011. In North America, perhaps incentivised by tax benefits, in 2015 the average lifetime charitable giving amongst this cohort represents 12% of their net worth. Other geographies are catching up; in Asia Pacific it is 10% and 9% in Europe, the Middle East and Africa.

As prosperity in the emerging economies continues to develop, countries that in the past have been the recipients of giving are now creating their own philanthropists. For example, Africa has around 165,000 super-rich people collectively worth over $660 billion. They have initiated a western-style, formalised philanthropy network across the continent. Aliko Dangote, the Continent's richest man, is taking the lead in encouraging Africa to help herself. He has already signed a pledge committing to give away a majority of his wealth to charitable causes. His Dangote Foundation is active in health, education and disaster relief.

India is also experiencing exponential growth in philanthropic giving with funding from private individuals recording a six-fold increase in

Growing ambition of global elite:

Tech pioneers in particular epitomise a new breed of philanthropist and have been tackling major challenges such as curing disease, combating world hunger and preparing for the impacts of epidemics, natural disasters and climate change. Philanthropic impact for many in this group is not just about writing a cheque, but also galvanising their considerable corporate resources and networks to help tackle major issues quickly and efficiently. However, although laudable in its intent, such is the scale of their ambitions and their perceived lack of accountability, some wonder whether this level of mega philanthropy is leading to an over concentration of power in the hands of a few.

Growing involvement of the global elite:

Extremely wealthy people who identify as philanthropists are shaping much of the social, political and even economic agenda. Some such as Warren Buffet, through his gifts to the Bill and Melinda Gates Foundation and Susan Thompson Buffet Foundation, do this overtly by promoting democratic values across the world, others such as Elon Musk use innovation to kick start brave new initiatives; he is a director of the X-Prize Foundation, which supports competitions to promote advances in clean energy. Until recently most of the global elite were from the US but increasingly this is no longer the case; they are also found in Africa and the East.

recent years.[x] Funds contributed by individual philanthropists have been steadily rising, growing faster than funds from foreign sources and funds contributed through corporate social responsibility. Some argue it is not before time, despite these great improvements and progressive government schemes such as Beti Bachao Beti Padhao, which focuses on female education, and Jan Dhan Yojana which promotes financial inclusion, there are still significant developmental barriers. Conservative estimates indicate that India will face a financial shortfall of approximately INR 533 lakh crore ($8.5 trillion) if it is to achieve the SDGs by 2030.

Many are working to address this – both in India and beyond. Indeed, it was observed in our London workshop which was hosted by the British Asian Trust and focused on the philanthropic role of the diaspora community, that as the centre of wealth shifts both East and South, and the international development budgets of the West continue to decline; the rich Asian and African diaspora, many of whom have retained strong connections, are placing an increasing amount of their philanthropic endeavours on their homeland in order to help others benefit from the opportunities they were given. The growing availability of new technology platforms, an increasingly global workforce and the ability to more easily target and engage with potential donors, will all continue this trend.[xi]

The rich Asian and African diaspora, many of whom have retained strong connections, are placing an increasing amount of their philanthropic endeavours on their homeland.

UBS / PWC Billionaires report

Billionaire wealth outperforms MSCI AC World Index in 2016

Figure 1: Wealth development of billionaires across the regions 1995–2016

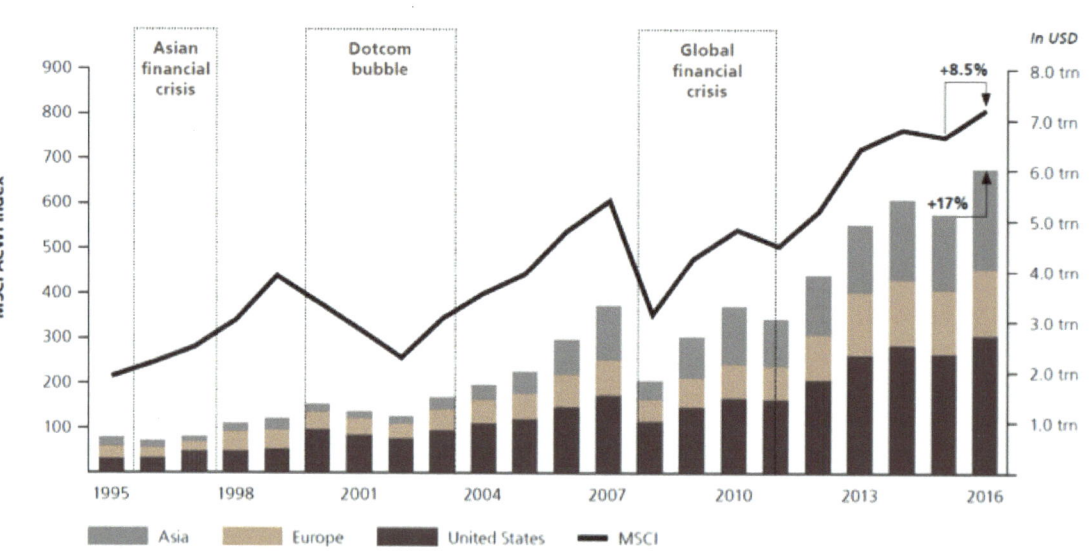

Asian wealth is increasing at a faster pace than in the US and Europe

Figure 4: Regional wealth dynamics 2016 billionaire cohort

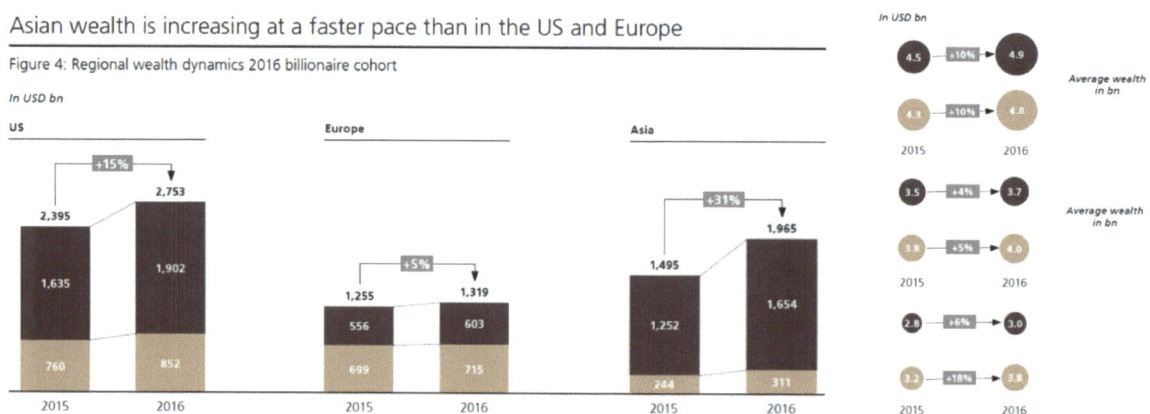

[Source: https://press.pwc.com/Multimedia/News-releases/All/ubs---pwc-billionaires-report-2017/a/34643eeb-7150-42a0-9cec-edac04bec92e]

Tech philanthropist mind-set - Big Bets

Nowhere is the impact of the new mind-set more evident than when we consider today's tech philanthropists. Rather than wait for proposals to come to them, they actively seek places to put their money. Having had phenomenal, world changing business success many are now focusing their attention on making it a better place. Unsurprisingly they prioritise speed and rapid impact. Bill and Melinda Gates define themselves as "impatient optimists working to reduce inequality". Again, this is not just an American phenomenon: Jack Ma in China, HCL founder Shiv Nadar and Infosys co-founder Gopalakrishnan in India are all examples of the new tech philanthropist, and in Europe, Virgin founder Sir Richard Branson has promised to invest in "entrepreneurial approaches to help make a difference to the world".

> Determined to see results in their own lifetimes, tech philanthropists are more willing to make big, often risky bets, with a focus on solving problems rather than serving needs.

Determined to see results in their own lifetimes, tech philanthropists are more willing to make big, often risky bets, with a focus on solving problems rather than serving needs. Wealth gives them the freedom to take risks. The Silicon Valley philanthropists, Facebooks's Dustin Moskovitz and his wife Cari Tuna, founders of Good Ventures have chosen to fund projects intended to mitigate potential global catastrophes, such as disease epidemic, biological warfare and the threats posed by advanced artificial intelligence. Lack of accountability to an electorate or shareholders makes failure perfectly acceptable. Indeed, the couple acknowledge that many of the projects funded by Good Ventures will not succeed, and are comfortable with that. "I actually expect that most of our work will fail to have an impact, and that is part of doing high-risk philanthropy well," Ms. Tuna has said.

A key component of the growth of big-bets philanthropy has been the emergence of higher risk innovative finance mechanisms that aim to provide risk capital to help reduce the $2.5 trillion annual funding gap needed to achieve the Sustainable Development Goals in developing countries alone. Diverse examples of this include the Rockefeller Foundation's Zero Gap initiative, the MacArthur 100 & Change challenge and The ImPact that aims to inspire super-wealthy families to make more impact investments more effectively. An example that captured media attention in 2018 was the Seychelles Governments protection of 210k sq m of the Indian Ocean in exchange for writing off some of its national debt. The finance came from several high net worths including Leonardo di Caprio working with The Nature Conservancy.

Despite all these good intentions some argue that all this is tokenistic, designed to take the focus away from past misdemeanors. Of particular irritation are the issues around tax, both from a payment perspective and also the suggestion that the tax breaks afforded to philanthropists may well be depriving the public sector of money that should be used to provide public services. Mark Zuckerberg and Pricilla Chan's pledge to use 99 percent of their Facebook shares to make the world a better place has come under particular criticism in this regard. Their creation of a limited liability

A sense of urgency: For an increasing number of philanthropists creating a legacy is no longer a priority and the focus has turned towards making an impact now. Some charitable foundations, many originally based on the idea of providing funding in perpetuity, are increasing their rate of spend and impact. In extreme cases, there is a shift of focus from maintaining and growing their endowment to committing to spend down; examples include the John Merck Fund in the US and the Gatsby Charitable Foundation in the UK.

The Rockerfeller Foundation's Zero Gap Initiative

Working at the intersection of finance and international development, Zero Gap is an example of how the development community can support and de-risk new and innovative financing mechanisms— including financial products and public- private partnerships— to mobilise large pools of private capital that have the potential to create out-sized impact. Employing a venture philanthropy model, the Zero Gap work supports early-stage research and design and leans heavily on collaboration and experimentation with both private and public sector partners. Zero Gap is focused on solutions that can ultimately catalyse large-scale capital from institutional investors, as well as household and retail investors.

company (LLC), the Chan Zuckerberg Initiative, rather than a charitable foundation as a base for donations is a relatively unusual step. LLCs offer greater control to the philanthropist but are less transparent than foundations because there's no obligation to provide information about their charitable work or its effectiveness. LLCs are free to invest their funds however they wish, including towards political causes. Avoiding both taxes and oversight, alongside continued allegations around Facebook's lack of transparency on corporate tax, has, for some, tarnished what otherwise would be one of the largest philanthropic pledges in history.

Some applaud these initiatives and point out that, because the super-wealthy and foundations are free of the constraints of regular reporting and so on, they can 'crack on', and in so doing find solutions to long term problems faster and more easily that governments or even corporates. Indeed, they argue, this approach might just be one of the best hopes for solving systemic problems such as the spread of disease, poverty and climate change or shorter-term, unpopular issues that may otherwise be ignored.

Others are not so sure and are concerned that, as the ambitions of these new philanthropists grow, so too does their influence. Having made their fortunes in creating social networks and building technology empires, whether we like it or not, soon these very same billionaires may have extraordinary unaccountable influence over all aspects of our lives from medical research, to education, to the delivery of social policy, politics and even the management of climate change.

> Given their tendency to support women's advancement, look out for a ripple effect. By helping other women succeed in the global economy female philanthropists are building the next wave of female donors.

In India the response has been to clampdown on an NGOs' ability to assert control over decision making in key policy areas. The country has also ordered the dismissal of dozens of foreign-funded health experts working on public welfare schemes. A unit of the Gates Foundation – funded Immunization Technical Support Unit (ITSU), which provides strategy and monitoring advice for New Delhi's massive immunisation programme that covers about 27 million infants each year, will now be funded by the government.

The Role of Women

Alongside the tech philanthropists, women are having an increasing influence in the field of high impact giving. Historically women have always been associated with good causes but recently we can see that they are changing where money is spent and there is a greater focus on helping other women. Some suggest that the number of female HNW philanthropists is accelerating not just because of the key underlying driver, that more women now control more wealth; for example 45% of

Limited Liability Companies

The scale and impact of some high-profile philanthropists including Mark Zuckerberg and Priscilla Chan, Pierre and Pam Omidyar and Warren Buffet has captured headlines and set ambitious goals for others to follow. Among this cohort there's a growing trend to create limited liability companies (LLCs) — such as the Chan Zuckerberg Initiative — rather than charitable foundations (a legal category of non-profit in the US) as a base for donations. LLCs offer greater control to the philanthropist although they don't share the same tax benefits. They are less transparent than foundations, because there's no obligation to provide information about their charitable work or its effectiveness. LLCs are also free to invest their funds however they wish, including towards political causes.

American millionaires are now women, but because many expect the new threats to gender equity, particularly under the Trump administration, will quicken the pace at which wealthy women choose to take a stand. A direct consequence of this is an increase in the number of women's funding networks. Women Moving Millions, a global community of mainly women donors, has more than doubled in size since launching, from 102 members in 2007 to 250 in 14 countries in 2017. Donors each give or pledge $1m or more to initiatives focused on advancing women and girls. Elsewhere, Impact Austin, a US giving circle — in which donors pool their funds — started in 2003 with six women, each donating $1,000 a year. It now has about 500 female members, who gave a total of $5m to charities in 2015.

According to the Women's Philanthropy Institute at Indiana University, women tend to spread their giving across several organisations whereas men typically concentrate on a narrower range of charities. Women are also more likely to volunteer — and volunteer more hours — than men. More modest by nature they also are inclined to take a low-profile role so their names are less likely to be prominent. Given their tendency to support women's advancement, look out for a ripple effect. By helping other women succeed in the global economy female philanthropists are building the next wave of female donors.

Local and Community Philanthropy

Coincident to the large-scale focus on causes rather than communities, we are also seeing a growing belief in grass-roots philanthropy initiatives. Community foundations, women's funds, environmental funds and other local grant-makers have all appeared in countries as diverse as Romania and Zimbabwe, Vietnam and Mexico. They have been shaped both by context and culture, and by individuals who are often distrustful of the relentless rise of globalisation.

Insights from Quito

Many of them are frustrated by the failures of traditional development aid, anxious about the sense of alienation and disenchantment in their communities that this has generated. They believe that without local resources, local leadership and local buy-in, development projects will be unable to deliver long term benefits. Although sometimes initially funded by an external grant, they all seek to build a culture of local philanthropy - and they deliberately use community grants as a way to strengthen and invest in the people around them.

The argument for this type of giving is that everyone has a stake in their local economy and therefore should 'chip in' whatever they can whether that be money, skill sharing, expert mentoring, child-care or some other kind of support. Examples from around the world include Pamoja4Change in Kenya, Tewa — a women's fund in Nepal, and the Dalia Association, the first Palestinian community foundation.

31

The growth of communities: Here 'community' action is taken in a narrow sense, epitomised by the local foundations appearing in a range of countries. These can be seen as a response to failures of traditional aid and public structures, but also, a reflection of an increase in self-referencing networks, with a distrust of 'outsiders' and increase in trust in 'people like me'. This aligns well to the creation of bottom-up community initiatives to tackle local issues.

Trust is a vital ingredient here – local initiatives work because the people involved know and support each other (notice they do not have to like each other). Each in some way have a clear responsibility for the wider community. This has growing appeal and in a world where trust is at a premium, the expectation is that these small-scale movements will proliferate. It is perhaps easy for some to scoff at such small- scale ambition but fans include former German president Horst Köhler, an economist by profession and a former president of the IMF.

The Missing Middle

The colossal clout of a small number of the largest charities can mean that the contributions of many smaller and medium sized non-profits can be under-estimated, with capital flowing accordingly. This is a perennial challenge. Smaller NGO's don't get as much philanthropic capital as the larger ones for many reasons including high transaction costs, limited capacity or overhead support to fund savvy fundraisers or even bank de-risking due to anti-money laundering or other regulation. More recently they have also come under additional pressure because of wide scale reductions in the state funding of philanthropic initiatives. Indeed, in Singapore it was suggested that some are already beginning to suffer. Often, at least in part manned by volunteers, they are less able to adapt to change and their limited resources, both in terms of funding and skills, make it almost impossible for them to evidence their work to attract further investment. The smaller the organisation the more difficult it becomes. And yet they are a vital part of civil society and work across communities delivering essential services.

This is particularly frustrating not least because it was observed that many larger non-profits gain funding despite the absence of reliable information about their relative performance. Many in our workshops agreed that billions of philanthropic dollars annually are distributed haphazardly among more than 1.5 million organizations, some deserving, some less so.

One remedy may lie in the celebrated "wisdom of crowds" – using the internet to get direct feed back on the design, implementation and impact of different initiatives from the very people who benefit from its activities. Many see this as a big change for the future. Certainly evidence at the 2017 Feedback Summit, which has a network of over 400 organisations, shows a growing trend amongst philanthropists to better close the feedback loop.

No other generation has entered the workforce with such high expectations of their employers. For them the barriers that used to separate life inside and outside the "office" simply don't exist

Millennial Shifts

From a demographic point of view, Baby Boomers currently are the greatest economic force in giving, and are expected to donate more than $6 trillion over the next 20 years. However, as they give way to the next generation, the rationale and focus of where and how to give is changing. In every workshop, in every location we visited it was clear that Millennials are about to take action. They are fed-up with the profligacy of their elders, recognise the need for change and are looking round for new and innovative ideas to make better things happen.

The next generation has grown to expect transparency, sophisticated storytelling and technical savvy from their charitable organizations.

They are also prepared to take action so many Millennial donors will not only give money, but will volunteer and lend the force of their own social networks to a cause they believe in. For this audience, issues like education, health care and the environment are top of mind, whereas institutional giving to traditional beneficiaries such as churches and established NGOs is less popular.

If you think we are exaggerating, think again. Research by Deloitte found that, across the globe, many millennials feel accountable for societal issues.[xiii] Those in developed nations, buffeted as they have been by economic and social stagnation, are less optimistic than their peers. That does not stop them trying to change the system however. Many believe that, although as individuals they are unable to exert any meaningful influence on the biggest global challenges, they can drive change through how and where they work and it is this that gives them a sense of empowerment. No other generation has entered the workforce with such high expectations of their employers. For them the barriers that used to separate life inside and outside the "office" simply don't exist. Philanthropy is integrated into their lifestyles. "Doing good" is directing their choice of career and employer as well as life choices, where and what they eat, what they wear, what they watch and other wider behaviours. They want to see their skills, networks and for-profit investments used as part of how they make an impact.

Increasingly, millennials integrate giving into their daily living, asking friends and family to sponsor a huge range of initiatives. They are prepared to pay more for a cup of coffee, a pizza or even their weekly shopping provided they know that a percentage is going towards a good cause. Many believe in self-directed giving by non-traditional forms including direct giving, impact investing and social involvement. They are the most likely cohort to support social entrepreneurs, who are using market-based models to tackle social problems, and believe that, rather than create dependencies, this is the most effective way of lifting people out of poverty.

They fight for causes rather than institutions and do not shy away from political issues such as LGBT rights or campaigns that challenge the establishment. They demand transparency, use social media to drive awareness. Their belief in action has fundamentally changed the philanthropy landscape.

Some profess scepticism in all of this, believing that the young in every generation are more optimistic, caring and proactive than their older, world-weary peers.

Clearly, we are generalizing - millennials, like any generation come in all shapes and sizes, good and bad. They are also the selfie-generation. Much can be made about their vanity, their short attention spans and the fact they are not yet burdened by the responsibilities of middle age but despite all this, a World Economic Forum study of 5,000 millennials surveyed in 18 different countries indicates that they still believe the top priority for any business should be, "to improve society."[xiv] Also, a professor at a leading US University told us that in his 35 years of teaching, he had never witnessed a generation so committed to improving the world. Looking ahead it's hard not to take hope from their mind-set, energy, enthusiasm and effort.

Insights from Washington DC

Theme 2: Knowledge

The second driver of change is knowledge and its practical application. A common complaint from donors is the lack of understanding around the real impact of a particular donation: "What has my money been used for and what difference has it really made?" Or, as we heard from one sovereign wealth fund, "we give away a lot of money, but we don't think we do it very well":

Sometimes the reason for this is simply down to manpower – there aren't enough people with the necessary skills to be able do the analysis. In addition, issues such as difficulties of attribution or the time-lag between intervention and results further complicate the matter. Donors can sometimes lack the information they need to understand the impact of their donation and to make informed decisions around future giving.

Donors increasingly expect to be able to follow their money, see change, and directly link results to the donation

Having said that, the collection of data is becoming increasingly possible and can help agencies understand how best to invest their limited resources. According to the U.N. Secretary-General's Independent Expert Advisory Group on the Data Revolution for Sustainable Development, "New technologies are leading to an exponential increase in the volume and types of data available, creating unprecedented possibilities for informing and transforming society." In addition, the impact that donations can have on individuals or specific projects can now be accurately monitored. This has the advantage of allowing donors direct access to the beneficiaries, cutting out any unintended third-party bias. This is one of the key drivers in the rise of data-driven philanthropy.

34

Data Driven Philanthropy

From UHNW individuals to social/media savvy Millennials, donors increasingly expect to be able to follow their money, see change, and directly link results to the donation. Importantly, this builds understanding, endless learning and provides information from which to improve impact. As Washington DC-based Feedback Labs REF (http://feedbacklabs.org/), a leader in this space says, "simply collecting feedback is not enough; closing the loop is what matters. Making regular people true co-creators in aid and philanthropy requires five steps: design, collect, analyse, dialogue, course correct. Creating buy-in among all stakeholders is crucial to completing all steps of the loop."

Certainly, access to more detailed information has transformed our understanding of the impact of philanthropy and shed greater light on how money flows, including where funds come from and how they are managed and disseminated. An increasing number of donors are able to accurately track their giving, helped by non-profit measurement sites such as Charity Navigator and GuideStar, and they can directly link results to the donation they have made. That said, there was scepticism in some quarters around the metrics that organisations such as these use, alongside their interpretation of what they consider to be deserving.

Despite these concerns, there was universal agreement that improved access to data can shift donating from being reactive and responsive to becoming more pro-active and impact driven, and ultimately helping all involved develop a more strategic and effective approach.

> There was universal agreement that improved access to data can shift donating from being reactive and responsive to becoming more pro- active and impact-driven

Better collection and use of data has other benefits alongside driving efficiency. It builds trust. Philanthropy, however well-meaning, is increasingly vulnerable to the public distrust and scepticism of the 'post-truth' society and as such the legitimacy, governance and practices of those involved is under growing scrutiny. In part, this is a self-inflicted wound as a recent slew of negative media stories have hit the headlines including allegations of financial mismanagement, damaging commercial relationships, aggressive fundraising activities and the abuse of power. These have tarnished a number of the high profile charities including Oxfam and the Red Cross. Increased transparency would help to address the problem, ensuring that good governance and accountability structures are in place. In addition, the standardisation of reporting would also help. But measuring the effectiveness of everything from protecting the environment to tackling world hunger on the same terms is tricky. New methodologies such as the Global Impact Investing Rating System (GIIRS) are emerging, but none is yet viewed as a panacea.

Despite its value in controlling efficiency and identifying bad practice, measuring the benefits of philanthropy is surprisingly hard. How can we measure "income" in a village of subsistence farmers or define the success of non-quantitative or non-monetary outcomes, like women's empowerment or entrepreneurial motivation?

Data driven philanthropy: Often enabled by digital technology, donors are increasingly able to follow their money, see change, and directly link results to their donation. Greater transparency enables more focus on areas that can make the most difference. However, the increasing dependency on data and the widespread sharing of personal information presents risks around privacy and freedom of expression. It also means that areas of need that are not 'measurable' may well be neglected.

Over the past decade, searching for a more rigorous approach, development researchers have applied the "gold standard" of medical research: randomised controlled trials (RCT). In a RCT, researchers allocate an intervention, such as a microfinance loan, to a randomly selected test group of people and compare their outcomes with a control group. This works well but RCTs are expensive and some baulk at the cost and suggest that sometimes there can too much emphasis on measurement and often this comes at the expense of innovation. Others point out that this is starting to change. For example, in Africa, researchers from the Massachusetts Institute of Technology's J-PAL — a network of academics from more than 50 universities — and non-profit group Innovations for Poverty Action, have been building the infrastructure for philanthropic RCTs. In addition, the World Bank, academics, and even some in the private sector are making impact measurement and survey data more freely available.

Despite this success, the drive for providing some form of quantified data on impacts has led to some elements of the charitable industry evolving into one that measures activities instead of outcomes. Too much measurement, it was suggested, has led to organisations taking fewer risks which has reduced their potential to find solutions to global problems.

The situation is exacerbated by lack of capacity. There are some very good smaller organisations that simply do not have the technology to gather data or the staff with the skills to interpret the results. The U.N. Secretary-General's Independent Expert Advisory Group on a Data Revolution for Sustainable Development points this out, "But, too many people, organizations, and governments are excluded [from the new world of data] because of lack of resources, knowledge, capacity, or opportunity." Looking ahead, as the cost of data collection and analysis fall and our understanding of how best to apply the insights it offers increases, it is hoped that more organisations, large and small, will benefit."

Emotional Giving vs. Effective Altruism

Measuring and monitoring the impact of a donation is clearly data-driven, but what about that first decision, the one where a potential donor chooses to engage with a cause or not? With limited resources, donors will give money to where they perceive it will have the most impact. This perception can be based on emotional intuition or a more quantitative approach.

Many begin their philanthropic journey with a personal connection to a specific cause. Although it may seem irrational, this strength of connection often has long-term value; history shows that donors generally engage longer with causes in which they are personally interested. Jeff Bezos, the entrepreneur founder of Amazon, uses some of his funds to support Mary's Place, a shelter for homeless women and children in Seattle, whose work Bezos said had, "inspired and moved" him. In the US only 3% of individuals compare organisations before making a donation and only 35% do research of any kind in making a philanthropic gift.[xvi]

Emotional motivations do not just affect individual donors. Even for larger donor organisations, which are subject to greater scrutiny and have more analytical tools at their disposal, the initial direction of giving is often based on a feeling rather than fact. Rati Forbes, head of Forbes Marshall Foundation, whose work is focused on improving urban sanitation explained, "I started out on this journey because things I saw moved me. So, for me, it started with

Although emotion may drive the initial choice of cause, for most donors, particularly those with a business background, some sort of quantified metrics, however sketchy, will be increasingly welcome when it comes to tracking the direction and impact of the gift.

the heart." However, once her interest was piqued, Rati became more focused, researching issues to understand where best to invest funds. This enabled her to choose to focus on sanitation at a time when funding toilets was almost unheard of in India.

The counter to this is that emotional giving poorly reflects relative causal need or the organization or mechanism that will make most impact for a selected cause. As such to have true impact donating "should" be guided by rational quantitative data. It is better to give to hospitals or schools rather than feel-good initiatives. Sentimentality, the argument goes, produces giving that is more self-indulgent for the donor than helpful.

Attitudes such as these have led to a growing interest in Effective Altruism (EA). This uses a quantified approach to ensure that donations achieve the greatest impact on the lives of those in need. Sometimes called "generosity for nerds", EA rejects personal concerns or interests and instead aims to find the most efficient ways to reduce suffering. This prescriptive approach can direct our goodwill in counter-intuitive ways. For example, if you want to devote your life to helping others, volunteering in children's homes or caring for the sick might not be your best bet. Instead, effective altruists could suggest you 'earn to give' and take a high-paying job because the disposable income you can donate will help more people than you could by simply volunteering in the field. Although considered harsh by some, this logical, data driven approach, has attracted support from high-profile fans like Elon Musk, Peter Thiel, Mark Zuckerberg and his wife, Dr. Priscilla Chan.

In truth, since no one donates without the intention of making a positive difference, most philanthropists, large or small, give on both an emotional and rational level. Although emotion may drive the initial choice of cause, for most donors, particularly those with a business background, some sort of quantified metrics, however sketchy, will be increasingly welcome when it comes to tracking the direction and impact of the gift.

Investing in Philanthropy Capacity

Charities are notoriously bad at investing in their own people and knowledge systems, either through fear of being considered profligate or because they simply don't have the available cash flow – as a result they may miss out on some much needed support. For example, some donors only consider giving to the larger foundations because they can benefit from their superior analytical and administrative resources. Some in our workshops even suggested that the reason that science and healthcare goals are well-represented is, in part, because of their data-oriented focus which appeals to many philanthropists, particularly those with previous business success.

To address this, one suggestion we heard was to create a "TripAdvisor" style website for doing good. This could outline the effectiveness of a charity's programmes and how it compares with other charities, and the views of the intended beneficiaries and/or other philanthropists.

Insights from Singapore

Collaborative Solutions

Sometimes the best investment a philanthropist can make is to help an organisation develop the core skills of the workers, and build the knowledge systems to grow and improve the impact of the organisation. An excellent example of this can be found in the methods of Humanitarian Leadership Academy. Spearheaded by Save the Children, it was set up to equip a new generation of humanitarians with the knowledge they need to prepare for, respond to and recover from crises', and aims to train 100,000 people from 50 countries by 2020. Operating globally, it facilitates partnerships and collaborative opportunities to enable people to prepare for and respond to crises locally by reaching out to those in the community who aren't professional humanitarians, but could play a vital role during a disaster, either because of where they live or the skills they have.

Initiated in 2015 it has built a web of connections across the globe opening centres in Central America, the Middle East, West Africa, Bangladesh, the Philippines and Indonesia, with more to follow over the next five years. Each centre makes a common pool of knowledge universally available and provides learning pathways for humanitarian workers, with internationally recognised certification, recorded in a 'humanitarian passport'.

This collaborative approach is expanding the pool of capable people available to prepare for and respond to an emergency and, alongside this, it is changing the face of the humanitarian sector, making aid quicker, cheaper, more efficient and effective.

Insights from London

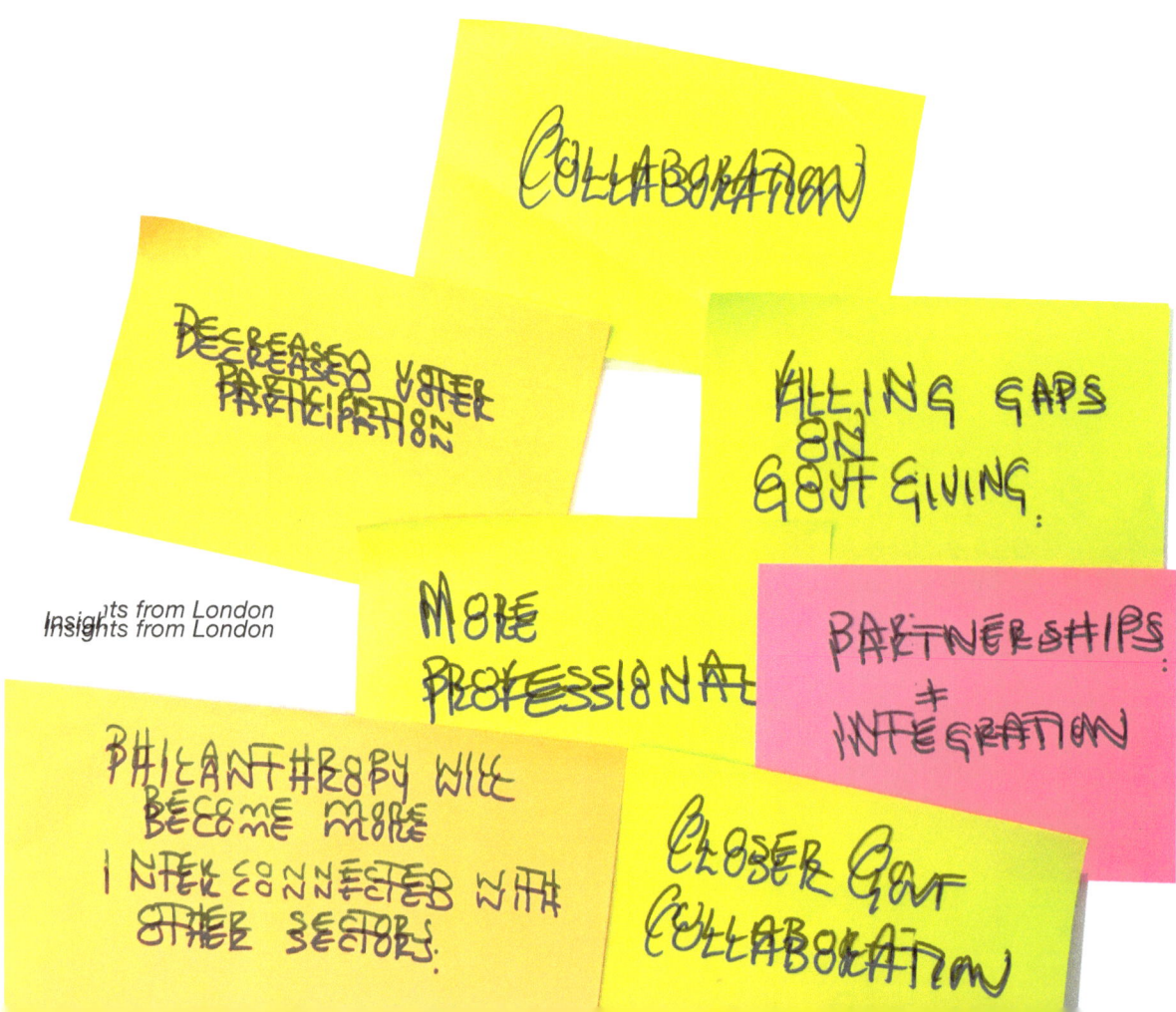

Collaborative giving: Donors are expanding their view of which groups can successfully develop solutions for society's challenges. Businesses, universities and religious institutions can work alongside NGOs and social enterprises shifting from operational silos and one-way partnerships to a more collaborative approach to fund raising, fund allocation and delivery. Charities, NGOs and businesses are more willing to collaborate and create shared value; policies are increasingly co-created by multiple parties, including government; there is growing cross-border sharing of best practice and successes; and, overall, duplication is being reduced leading to greater impact per unit of spend.

Broader collaboration and technology driven transparency were common themes in many of our discussions, with both seen to be increasingly important in the future. A good example is the collaboration between The Mastercard Center and DataKind, which works on social impact projects in U.S. cities and globally. As DataKind founder and CEO Jake Porway explains, "data is in abundant supply, but human capital is scarce."

The range of social impact projects that the data science teams tackled included initiatives correlating disease and scarcity of food sources in Africa, teaming up with the Red Cross to reduce fire deaths in America, and working with a community college to track drop out and success rates.

Thankfully there are many further examples of successful collaborations to learn from. The Asia P3 Hub in Singapore is a World Vision-led incubator that works with companies, start-ups and non-profit organisations to build strategic, mutually beneficial partnerships and bring about transformational change within communities across Asia Pacific. In Malaysia, Think City is a community-focused urban regeneration organisation that aims to create more livable, resilient and people-centric cities. Also, when Jack Ma, founder of e-commerce giant Alibaba, wanted to foster environmental sustainability in China, he organised a group of other like-minded entrepreneurs to collaborate and created the Paradise International Foundation, which focuses on nature conservation. Finally, in the Middle East, the Pearl Initiative founded by Badr Jafar, CEO of Crescent Enterprises; and Amir Dossal, Founder & Chairman of Global Partnerships Forum; bring together private sector business leaders from across the Gulf Region to create and adopt higher standards of corporate accountability.

The desire for broader collaboration and partnerships for impact can sometimes be a bumpy journey as evidenced by the 2% CSR law in India. Some suggest that it is partially designed to encourage collaboration, private public partnerships and the like, while others, particularly those in our Mumbai workshop, felt that in its current form, it does quite the opposite. Many predict that over time this will have to be modified, especially as private companies seek to have more international links.

Looking ahead expect more collaborative approaches which expand the pool of capable people available to prepare for and respond to need — and make philanthropy quicker, cheaper, more efficient and effective. Despite the growth in collaborative initiatives there was a widespread belief that we are moving towards greater fragmentation in some areas. This is a consequence of the increase in direct giving and the growing concentration of wealth in the hands of the few. An emerging issue is how large-scale private donor engagement is beginning to bypass established philanthropic initiatives.

Learning from Stories

In the pursuit of hard, empirical data, individuals and their stories may be lost in a flurry of numbers. But these stories are a form of knowledge too as is evidenced by the growth in direct giving and crowdfunding platforms which has not only made it easy to contribute but also to share and be inspired by personal human stories which help connect individuals to the people and causes they care most about. A strong beneficiary voice can lend legitimacy to the approach and intervention.

Culture has long been a conduit for advocacy and new technologies are now allowing increasingly immersive media approaches to add richness and colour. A strong supporter of this is Alejandro Linarite, the Oscar-winning director of "The Revenant". He created "Carne y Arena" ("Flesh and Sand") a virtual reality project that replicates the experience of migrants making the perilous journey across the Sonoran desert into America. Users are placed amongst a group of digitally-rendered migrants—all dehydrated, wounded, exhausted— and witness the harsh spotlights of helicopters overhead and the force of border control agents. Other examples include the Partnership between the United Nations and the Here Be Dragons virtual reality production company, which focused on a mother whose children were killed in the 2014 Israel-Gaza conflict, and a 12-year-old girl living in the Za'atari refugee camp. Both these examples create empathetic engagement and connection to the cause. All this would suggest that virtual reality is an ideal fundraising tool. Certainly, so far it has been very effective; "Clouds Over Sidra" the Here Be Dragons's Za'atari experience, was part of a UN humanitarian appeal that raised $3.8bn.

The technology is just taking off and augmented reality, which projects images onto the real world, may well be swift to follow. Gaming, too, offers new ways to connect for creative philanthropists: "Playmob", a platform that connects game developers with charities, claims to have fed 10,000 families and saved 31 pandas.

Future Role of the Media

Supporting positive social change has long been in the remit, and included in the programming content, of organisations such as NPR and the BBC.[xviii] However, adjacent to improved storytelling, there has also been increased interest and participation from the media in creating an appetite for positive change. A 2017 example from the UK is the role of the media in Heads Together[xix], an initiative that sees The Duke and Duchess of Cambridge and Prince Harry working to eliminate stigma around mental health. Other initiatives highlighted in the Mumbai workshop included Breakthrough TV, the depiction of a child bride in the soap opera Balika Vadhu and the encouragement of greater social activism through the Tata Tea Jaago Re adverts.

Social-media has now also become a force for social development. In China, WeChat and AliPay have created online markets for agricultural goods, enabling service providers to engage with their users, and raising funds to support humanitarian assistance programs such as drought relief in South Africa or earthquake recovery in Sichuan province.[xx]

Looking ahead, workshop participants were clear that there will need to be more, deeper and ongoing media engagement and there was much discussion about how this could be achieved. At the same time, social networks are increasingly allowing NGOs to by-pass traditional intermediaries and reach the public directly. The 2014 ice bucket challenge was a phenomenon of the summer. People dunked a bucket of iced water over their heads in order to solicit donations before nominating others to do the same. Although few were even aware of which cause they were supporting, the campaign raised over US$100 million over a 30-day period for ALS.[xix]

Insights from London

Theme 3: Trust

The final driver of change is trust. Philanthropy and philanthropists have always been vulnerable to public scepticism, and in many countries government scepticism too, but recently the distrust is growing.

In part, this is the unintended consequence of earlier approaches where generally the well-intentioned developed initiatives without having much constructive dialogue with the recipients of their benevolence. It is also a public reaction to the fact that a small group of people, who have made more money than they need, seem to have decided to invest substantially in issues that affect us all without our consent. With names like Soros, Gates, Bloomberg, Mercer, Koch and Zuckerberg, this team of mega-donors has driving ambition to get things done and their desire for results is upending philanthropic norms.

Some find this particularly concerning from a democratic perspective. They believe we are now looking at a future when the holders of private wealth are able to re-shape society according to their own philosophy with little or no accountability and we are witnessing the emergence of a philanthropic oligarchy, where rich individuals, who do not need to answer to shareholders or the democratic process, can quite literally re-shape the world. See for example the 2018 FT article "Elon Musk and the silly billy billionaire's club" Indeed, often their influence now extends way beyond national boundaries.

Worse, the growing trend towards anonymous philanthropy, with more donors opting for opaque DAFs and LLCs as their giving vehicles can blanket the whole process in secrecy. Others believe these worries are overplayed. After all there are often very good reasons for anonymity – not least to protect vulnerable beneficiaries or indeed to avoid unnecessary media harassment. But, when donors use their gifts to sway public policy or interfere in international issues, most in our workshops agreed that it is important to know who they are.

42

We are now looking at a future when the holders of private wealth are able to re-shape society according to their own philosophy with little or no accountability and we are witnessing the emergence of a philanthropic oligarchy, where rich individuals, who do not need to answer to shareholders or the democratic process, can quite literally re-shape the world.

Such is the size and scale of some philanthropic initiatives, particularly those from the US, it is understandable that some governments are distrustful of the over involvement of what they see as a modern form of colonialism. India is particularly sensitive in this regard. Around 11,000 non-governmental organizations have lost their licenses to accept foreign funds since Prime Minister Narendra Modi took office in 2014. Major Western funders — among them George Soros's Open Society Foundations and the National Endowment for Democracy — have been barred from transferring funds without official permission.

Clearly if they are to achieve their goals change-making philanthropists must build and maintain trust in the communities in which they operate. This applies at both national and local level. The challenge is how to achieve this, especially at scale, and particularly in contemporary society where trust in any of the established organisations is already at historical low ebb.

Those we spoke to referred to the need to address three elements:

- Integrity, the ability to act transparently and democratically;
- Reliability, the ability to act consistently — even when times are tough; and
- Competence, the ability to deliver results.

Trust in NGO's in decline; Edelman Trust Barometer 2017

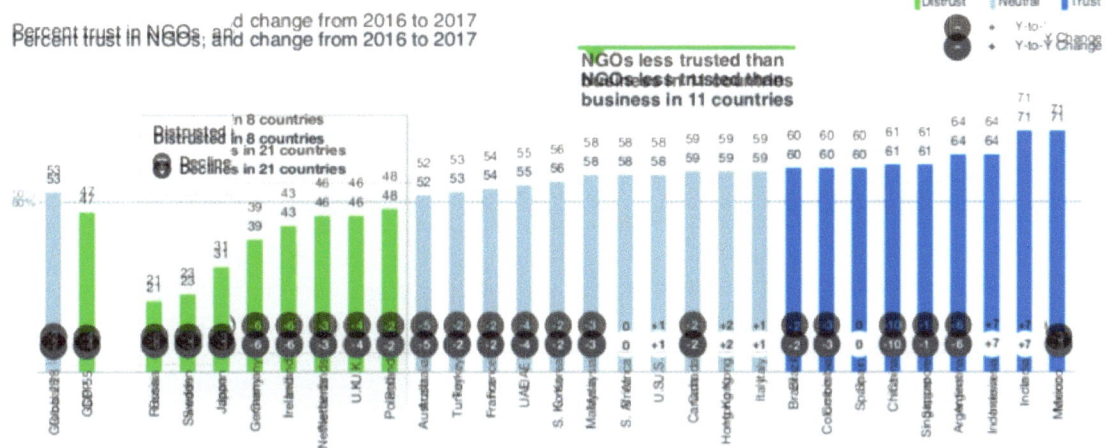

Source: https://www.edelman.com/global-results/

Sticky notes:
- FOCUS ON TRUST
- NON PROFIT PARTNERSHIPS DRIVE POSITIVE CHANGE
- PRIVATE PHILANTHROPY HAS LESS CHECKS + BALANCES → BUT GROWING ;-)
- BALANCE PROFIT WITH RESPONSIBILITY
- The challenge to philanthropy by populist backlash will cause a debate on corporate + income tax systems. It may also deter or shift personal philanthropy
- BLURRED LINE BETWEEN CHARITY + BUSINESS → SOCIALLY MINDED BUSINESS
- Business as social change incubators.

> Even philanthropists need to ensure they admit when they are wrong.

Insights from Oxford

Integrity

Simply stating that an organisation is acting with integrity is not enough to gain trust. Organisations must earn it by actually doing something worthwhile effectively and consistently. A stated purpose and direction does much to set parameters but is only a start. Increasingly, the appetite is for actions to be recorded and measured so that there is more transparency around their impact. Used correctly technology is a huge help. Indeed some argue that the greater transparency it enables, the more trust can be built. But it's not a given; there is huge scepticism around whether impact measurement is either possible or even cost effective. Clearly those who are interested can follow the money, and may even witness change, but often it is almost impossible to make a direct link. The British Heart Foundation, for example, is clear that it is only one player in the measurable reduction of heart disease.

Clear communication and proactive collaboration are also key indicators that an organisation is acting with integrity. So is listening. One way of gathering feedback in a constructive way is through closed feedback loops in which all stakeholders actively participate. This offers donors the ability to build and adapt programmes as the circumstances change and the effect of their initiatives are better understood within communities.

Even philanthropists need to ensure that they admit when they are wrong. If they don't, they create concern not only about integrity but about competence too. Mark Zuckerberg, learnt this lesson the hard way when it emerged that his $100m donation to transform the schools in Newark had failed. He is trying again in the San Francisco Bay area, but this time he has taken a more collaborative approach. He is working with a local support base and through them is building a constituency prepared to take action and get others to think, engage with and care about the cause. Hopes are high that this time he will be successful. It is much harder to designate an organisation as an arrogant outsider when its supporters include those who live in the area.

More broadly, the significance of trust in philanthropy goes a long way to explain why there is such a growth in community philanthropy initiatives and local giving circles . Unlike their global equivalents, local organisations are able, bit by bit, to build trust within, between and among the people they serve, not only through the transparent stewardship and flow of resources, but also by deliberately fostering multiple relationships at the local level including between those who have resources and can be convinced to give, those who have ideas and aspirations and for whom a small grant can make all the difference and those who for the first time are made to realise that they too possess useful assets.

Increasing the power of the beneficiary voice also assists in growing the legitimacy of the approach and intervention. This is one of the reasons why crowd funding has had such an impact. Crowd funding is often driven by grass-roots initiatives and can sometimes challenge many existing institutional delivery models, which historically have taken a paternalistic approach to giving, urging people to listen instead to what beneficiaries really want. Crowd funding is challenging the very process of philanthropy, with some foundations choosing to share the power and decision-making over where and how their philanthropic dollars are spent with those who are directly affected. This mandating of donations, as practiced by the Open Society Foundations, improves both legitimacy and transparency. The critical benefit here may be the increased and enduring sense of ownership of the solutions created, something that arguably the social entrepreneur movement has long been aware of.

Importantly crowdfunding also gives beneficiaries their own platform. As Kevin Johnson writes in Non-Profit Quarterly, "Much of the DNA of today's non-profit sector is based on a cultural history that might be summarised by the phrase, 'We're experts. Trust us, give us money and we'll do the right work.' The premise of crowdfunding starts from the exact opposite point of view — that beneficiaries know best about what they need and how to spend it. It's not just another fundraising tool; rather, it's a vibrant new life form."

Regular, interactive communication with stakeholders is also critical and builds trust. Listening to others is as important as broadcasting intent. This may explain why Amazon CEO Jeff Bezos is attempting to crowd source his philanthropic activities. He turned to his Twitter account for suggestions on where his money and efforts would be best directed stating, "This tweet is a request for ideas". It is an interesting beginning to his next philanthropic journey and, assuming he follows up with some of the recommendations that it has stimulated, may well ensure that his future activities are given greater support.

By encouraging "ordinary" people to give and feel as though they have a stake, these collaborative organisations offer essential spaces to build voice, resources and power and in so doing legitimise philanthropy as relevant for us all.

Reliability

In addition to those with faith, religious charities attract significant donations from non-believers. In an increasingly secular world one reason for this is that they offer a tried and tested route to philanthropic giving. For many, they can be relied on to "do good". As we are currently living in a time of intense change many are keen to hang on to the steady standards they believe that religion offers which have been established over centuries.

Similarly, the 'BINGOs' - the Big International NGOs - are seen by many as a reliable, safe bet. The likes of World Vision and MSF all have high levels of professionalism and strong track records that give a strong sense of on-going reliability. However this perspective is not universal and in some of our events, concerns were expressed about the integrity and reliability of some international organisations at a national level. Indeed, in some cases BINGOs are viewed as part of the problem and are being challenged by the emergence of more nimble, adaptive and efficient high-growth start- ups. Like a huge tanker trying to change course, BINGOs can be seen as slow to react and weighed down by bureaucracy. High profile examples of their inefficiencies seem to prove the point and include the Red Crescent in Yemen, Oxfam in Haiti and The American Red Cross' failure to react effectively during the Haiti hurricane. They are of course not alone in allegedly spending too much money on consultants and too little on direct aid but their size and scale makes them an easy target for media attention. An alternative approach to their dominance is now evidenced by the growing influence and impact of social entrepreneurs supported by organisations such as Ashoka and the Skoll Foundations.

In some cases, BINGOs are viewed as part of the problem and are being challenged by the emergence of more nimble, adaptive and efficient high-growth start-ups.

Community philanthropy and the Bezos example demonstrate that trust is more easily established if built on connections with real people than with organisations. This distinction explains why many philanthropists now bypass third-party media and use direct links such as Twitter, Facebook and the like, to talk to their communities.

Looking ahead, as social media allows every individual to effectively be their own media company many see that there is less need to rely on the likes of CNN or the BBC to represent them and instead become their own broadcaster, sharing news and ideas with a self selected community. That is of course if they can differentiate themselves from the noise of others doing the same thing.

Competence

Many of the new philanthropists believe that they have already demonstrated competency in their professional lives, however they recognise that this alone does not necessarily equip them for the wider social challenges they are likely to face when they get involved in the non-profit world. Given the current lack of accountability, greater transparency, robust governance structures and clear reporting processes are key to building trust. This may explain why there is growing support for the development of standardised philanthropic reporting and an acknowledgement in some quarters that independent organisations which evaluate philanthropy, such as GuideStar, GiveWell and Charity Navigator, also have an important role to play. Technical solutions, such as the increased use of blockchain may in the future also help primarily as an enabler. Although it was recognised that "it won't in itself give us trust, but it might give us transparency."

Philanthropy Advisors are also playing an increasingly important role in enabling and accelerating competence. There will always be a group of philanthropists for whom a large part of the fulfilment is in finding their own causes and charities to support.

But according to a 2017 report by The Philanthropy Workshop around 9% of high and ultra high net worth individuals are using philanthropy advisory services that go beyond the scope of traditional financial advisors for whom charitable giving is considered from a tax perspective rather than in a wider social context. Such a professional teaches and empowers their clients to direct their philanthropic resources effectively, becoming a 'one stop shop' for all the complexities of giving including identifying opportunities, information gathering, strategy and programme planning, and grants management in a multi-year giving programme. They deliver huge value to individual donors or smaller foundations by, for example, allowing funders to pool their money behind sophisticated grant-making strategies. Specialist advisors can also provide expertise in project management, which is much needed when facilitating collaboration across diverse philanthropy partners.

Trust is vital to this relationship and prospective philanthropists should choose their advisors wisely. Inexperienced but expensive consultants whose backgrounds are in finance as opposed to the social sector abound.

The Changing Ways to Give

It is no surprise that wealthy and well-connected people, in particular business men and women, may decide that establishing their own charity is the most effective way for them to deliver the highest impact. Usually they have considered their options and decided that, rather than give to inefficient organisations, their money could be put to better use remaining in their own control and benefitting from the skills and acumen that enabled them to build their fortunes in the first place.

Many giving mechanisms have existed for decades, such as volunteering, workplace giving, giving circles and the pooling of funds in local communities. However, the last decade or so has seen a blossoming of new ways to give and a rise in any number of philanthropy advisors who can help the undecided make up their minds as to how and where to put their money. Not only this but we have also seen the rise of global targets and frameworks, such as the Sustainable Development Goals which, although not a philanthropic giving vehicle in the strict sense, have provided a sign post for many to focus their interest.

The logistical ways in which we can give have become increasingly creative; at one end we see the growth of Impact Investing and Donor Advised Funds (DAFs) and at the other crowd-funding. Looking ahead, as the demands for transparency grow, and there is increased fear of corruption, either real or perceived, expect more criticism and even regulation around how money is raised and the way it is distributed.

> Looking ahead, as the demands for transparency grow, and there is increased fear of corruption, either real or perceived, expect more criticism and even regulation around how money is raised and the way it is distributed.

The United Nation's Sustainable Development Goals (UNSDG's)

In order to find an appropriate focus, many experienced donors begin their analysis of issues at a high level, with very big subject areas or abstract problems:

UN Sustainable Development Goals Source

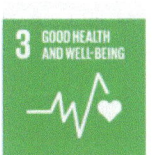

Source: http://www.un.org/sustainabledevelopment/sustainable-development-goals/

poverty, disease education and climate change, for example. The United Nation's (UN's) original eight Millennium Development Goals, with their specific targets, have helped focus efforts as they provide valuable alignment for action. Indeed, some suggest that providing a crystallised point for philanthropic and government funding priorities has been one of their most successful roles. Certainly many agree that the focus they provided in the provision of health care, for example, has meant that international development assistance in this area more than trebled after the year 2000, with the creation of new multilateral agencies and bilateral funding commitments towards maternal and child health and infectious diseases.

Launched in 2015, the UN's updated 17 Sustainable Development Goals (SDGs) cover a huge range of challenges including ending poverty, transforming health and education, improving our cities and communities, addressing gender equality, and tackling climate change. Collectively, they propose a new development pathway, based on partnership between governments, civil society and business that, if successful, could transform our societies.

However, during our workshops there was concern that the increase in the number of the development goals, from eight to 17, and of the specific targets, from 18 to 169, risks reducing the strength of focus for future effective collaboration and action. There was also concern that the identified investment gap of $3tn annually was not being filled by the private sector. Fewer than half of the world's global companies plan to engage with the goals, according to Ethical Corporation's "State of Responsible Business 2016" report.

Most workshop participants believed that the SDGs need to better align private sector incentives with sustainable development objectives through strengthened policies and sound institutional, legal and regulatory frameworks if there was to be any hope of ensuring their achievement. On the other hand, the SDGs were also criticised for their success, with some workshop attendees suggesting that such is their profile within the media and clout within the political environment that other issues are falling through the cracks.

Impact Investing

Harnessing capitalism and capital markets to promote change is in vogue and growing rapidly. Impact investing - investing in assets that offer measurable social or environmental benefits as well as financial returns - is becoming an increasingly popular way of being both philanthropic and profitable. So much so in fact that several establishment names including Goldman Sachs, UBS, BlackRock and TPG, with its $2Bn Rise Fund, have all recently launched impact funds. The sector has been boosted by increased attention from policy makers and the development of industry standards. Foundations too are following suit. The Ford Foundation has put aside $1Bn for mission or impact investing. As Darren Walker, the Foundation's CEO puts it, "it's not just 5 per cent of your money you give away that matters. What you do with the other 95 per cent is almost more important."

Impact Investing has also been endorsed by international organisations such as the UN. A UBS white paper, launched at Davos in 2017, argued that supporting affordable and clean energy and climate action are the two Sustainable Development Goals that can benefit most from private investment. At a time when low interest rates around the world have made financial returns harder to find, 75 percent of respondents said that the performance of their impact investments had met or exceeded their expectations. A 2017 Financial Times "Investing for Global Impact" report, which surveyed 246 family offices and foundations about philanthropy and impact investing, found almost a fifth said they were targeting a gain of more than 15 per cent over the next 12 months and more than a tenth were aiming for between 11 and 15 per cent.

Looking ahead the use of Environmental Social and Governance (ESG) is expected to grow. As better data becomes available for impact investing, its use by larger foundations may enable the establishment of standards and processes that assist smaller foundations in being able to engage in this practice while performing the measurement and analysis that will increasingly be expected by both donors and regulators.

Donor Advised Funds

A controversial, but increasingly popular, way of giving is through donor-advised funds (DAFs). These allow philanthropists to make a contribution to a fund and receive the tax deduction immediately. The funds do not have to be disbursed to charities until later. Certainly DAFs are becoming hugely popular in the USA, increasing from about 180,000 in 2010 to over 270,000 in 2015, with assets doubling in value in that time to roughly $80bn. Unlike foundations, they do not have to make annual donations, which means some fear that they are increasingly being used as a way of avoiding tax. Some in our workshops also pointed out that it was not clear whether DAFs actually increase the amount of money that reaches the needy and suggested that the tax breaks associated with them mainly benefit the rich. DAFs certainly lack transparency. Recent research by The Economist found that although many payments went to worthy causes such as Médecins Sans Frontières and the Red Cross, the biggest recipient of DAFs' gifts is Fidelity Charitable, a non-profit linked to the mutual-fund group. Another worry, particularly in the US, is the use of DAFs to circumvent the "public-support test". This stipulates that a charity typically must receive the lion's share of its revenue from the general public. A creative donor could donate to a charity through numerous DAFs, giving the false impression of widespread public support. Last year, the IRS announced an investigation into this.

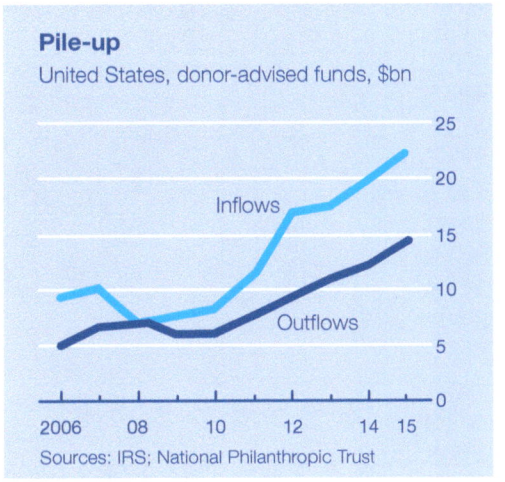

Pile-up
United States, donor-advised funds, $bn
Sources: IRS; National Philanthropic Trust

Venture Philanthropy

For wealthy millennials, particularly those with business backgrounds who aim for the same efficiency in their giving as in their work, "impact driven philanthropy" and "venture philanthropy, modelled on venture capitalism, have gained rapidly in appeal. Both offer ways to invest in charities that are data driven and demand more accountability as to the effectiveness of the donation. Both are testing new approaches to solving old problems. Some big donors, including the Gates Foundation and USAID, the American government's international aid agency, run competitions for innovative approaches, which are extended if they prove to be effective and efficient. They look for rigorous evaluation and expect results. But demanding proof of impact is not necessarily always the right approach. For example, as with business, it may push charities to focus on easy-win short-term outcomes, rather than more meaningful long-term measures of success. Furthermore, risky projects, such as working with persistent offenders or on funding medical research initiatives might suffer.

Family Foundations

If you are wealthy the most popular way to give is still to set up a foundation which can exist in perpetuity, investing their endowments and giving out a percentage of the returns each year. However changing attitudes to giving are shaping when and how money is donated. Younger donors, particularly high net worth individuals, are noticeably keen to make a difference in their lifetime rather than waiting to the end of their career. Many have adopted new models of giving for example by engaging in public-private partnerships and impact investing, the leveraging of private capital for public good. Some also spoke of the potential emergence of outsourced 'virtual foundations', replacing the need and cost of individuals choosing to create their own.

Crowdfunding

Crowdfunding is the new kid on the block in terms of raising funds and yet it has had huge impact – not only by enabling deeper and more sustained engagement with individuals but also by engaging with wider movements of people seeking to create or contribute to positive change and to do so transparently. Used as a tool of both direct giving and raising donations for charities, crowdfunding allows pretty much anyone with a laptop and a bit of connectivity to quickly start and share a campaign for any imaginable social issue, funnelling the proceeds directly to the recipient.

In the commercial world, we are familiar with how crowdfunding platforms have already shifted how entrepreneurs and new ventures raise capital and secure support from future customers for their endeavours, with platforms such as Kickstarter that has raised more than $3Bn for 130,000 projects, and equity crowdfunder Seedrs. The same has also been true in the fundraising world, with social fundraising platforms such as JustGiving (raised more than $4.5Bn) and GoFundMe (raised more than $3Bn from 25 million donors). The strength of these platforms is not only in their ability to make it easy to contribute but also in using individual and social data to help connect individuals to the people and causes they care most about. An example of this is the level of integration between the JustGiving and Facebook platforms.[xxvi]

Crowdfunding works particularly well in 'response causes,' with powerful stories including news events, local appeals and disaster relief requests. Activist organisations can also benefit from mobilising new money quickly and bypassing slow-moving or conservative foundations. While luck and the media determine who benefits from a campaign gone viral, an emotional appeal tends to be the key ingredient of success.

The wider impact of this new way of fundraising is both a shift in who the funders are, how that work gets done and by whom. The crowd is not only being leveraged for the giving of money, it is also being used to access individuals' time and talent. One example of such crowdsourcing for philanthropy is Cancer Research UK's "Citizen Science" programme[xxvii] which has accessed and enabled over 500,000 people from 182 countries to join forces and accelerate research into the prevention and cure of cancer.

Perhaps as importantly is the enhanced ability of people to take ownership and create impactful change themselves.[xxviii] There is no need to wait for governments or large international NGOs. Individuals and small groups are now more easily able to organise amongst themselves and raise funds, as epitomised by the long-standing Harambee movement in Kenya.[xxix] For many this is liberating, and yet this sort of informal, reactive and emotional approach does not sit comfortably with strategic giving. Some critics point to "slacktivism" arguing the overall impact has been small – most contributors don't give regularly and donations are generally below $50. Looking ahead many agree that there is much still to learn and that is an opportunity for crowd-based philanthropy mechanisms to be more strategic and to achieve this crowd funding platforms must become more specific.

Many agree that there is much still to learn and that is an opportunity for crowd-based philanthropy mechanisms to be more strategic.

Going Direct

Many in our workshops also saw the logistics of giving changing as philanthropy becomes focused on individuals directly rather than being channeled through charities. As is evident in many other walks of life, from accommodation (e.g. Airbnb) to transport (e.g. Uber), the drive to cut out the middleman and increase efficiency offers potential in philanthropy too. While direct philanthropy has always existed (think of simply giving to the needy on the street), the shift enabled by digital technology makes it easier, faster and, critically, independent of geography.

> While direct philanthropy has always existed (think of simply giving to a beggar on the street), the shift enabled by digital technology makes it easier, faster and, critically, independent of geography.

Alongside coins, and cheques in the mail, credit cards, payroll giving points, Apple Pay and even bitcoins are widely available. Mobile money has been transformative in this regard. As long ago as 2011, 'Kenya for Kenyans' raised £6m from 250,000 individuals to provide famine relief to over 3 million Kenyans. Backed by leading telecoms company, Safaricom, a rapid awareness campaign coupled with the MPesa mobile payments platform quickly brought in contributions. A similar appeal has been made to combat Ebola in West Africa and the Garissa attacks in Kenya also saw widespread use of mobile in fundraising for victims.

Direct donations are particularly effective when used to tackle poverty and financial exclusion at source. GiveDirectly has given more than $100m in unconditional direct cash transfers to the poor with 91% of all monies reaching the end user.xxx Kiva, which uses repayment finance has lent over $1Bn to 2.5m borrowers in 83 countries with a 97% repayment rate.xxxi This level of micro-finance delivered with mobile payments technology enables donations to reach extremely poor families in the most capital efficient way currently possible.

Studies have also found that giving directly can be more effective than indirect approaches. Direct philanthropy appears to lend itself to tighter evaluation and feedback loops, which drive increased efficiency and impact over time. For example, a Princeton-led randomised control study showed that GiveDirectly's approach in Kenya increased earnings by $270, increased household assets by $430 and nutrition spend by $330, with zero increase in tobacco and alcohol use.xxxii So successful has this approach been that in late 2017 GiveDirectly launched a $30m Universal Basic Income initiative to give basic incomes to thousands of recipients in Kenya. Moreover, the direct approach can also facilitate storytelling between recipients and donors (e.g. www.live.givedirectly.org/ www.kiva.org/about/impact/success-stories):

The impact of personal giving: Increased transparency, new technologies and the ability to make small donations conveniently and securely have dramatically changed the way individuals give and their ability to understand the impact of their donation. From technical solutions such as Just Giving, GoFundMe and Global Giving to direct impact donations through Kiva and GiveDirectly, as well as increased corporate support through workplace giving initiatives and matched donations, the public have multiple ways of becoming aware of, involved in and making a contribution to issues they care about.

The efficiency of Direct Philanthropy is alluring and clearly has the potential to challenge existing giving models. For example, the Brookings Institute calculates that it would cost $70Bn per annum to get everyone in the world above the poverty line and yet we currently spend $135Bn each year on global aid. While this analysis is of course overly simplistic, many would argue that at the very least it provides a benchmark for efficiency. Interestingly, leading global NGOs such as Oxfam are now experimenting with more direct approaches such as loading cash directly onto a card to buy essential provisions like rice, eggs, oil and wheat for the most vulnerable in Iraq.xxxiii

Concluding Thoughts

Philanthropy is not a new phenomenon but it is at different stages of maturity around the world. Similarly, our individual and collective philanthropic motivations, goals, approaches, ability to assess impact and degree of involvement differ.

As highlighted earlier, Schumpeter's waves of creative destruction, powered by the digital technologies that define our era, are expected to ensure that over the next decade changes in philanthropy, as elsewhere, accelerate. As societal attitudes, behaviours and commercial common sense adjust and align to a connected and data driven digital world, so will philanthropy.

Digital technology enables both atomisation and collaboration. A positive view might be that as society seeks to address the underlying causes of social and environmental challenge, longer- term systemic and broader collaborative solutions will come to the fore. A more jaundiced view may assert that short-term self-interest and increasing polarisation will ensure that societal divides and environmental destruction will continue to worsen.

Leadership, be it from Government, the global elite or from crowd-powered citizens will guide the outcome. Positive use of Power, Knowledge and the earning and retention of the Trust of all stakeholders will be vital to success.

Questions for the Future

As we move forward, there are clearly many issues impacting the future of philanthropy. Some of these will drive change for donors, charities, intermediaries and for corporates. Others will require action by governments and regulators. Below are a series of questions that could be considered in the planning of a future agenda.

Five Questions for Donors:
- What **impact** do I wish to have with my gift?
- What **specific area** that I support can have the greatest influence over the future?
- Given all the options, who can I **best support and why** to create most impact?
- Which of **my daily choices** can play a part in changing the status quo?
- How can I **get involved** or who can I collaborate with to have even greater impact?

Five Questions for Charities
- What is the most powerful role that we can **uniquely play** to help set the most impactful agenda in our chosen field?
- Who should we **collaborate with across the spectrum** to have more lasting impact?
- What actions can we take to increase **our legitimacy** and become more transparent and so more open to public scrutiny?
- How can we better **access, create, use and share our and others' data** to deliver more impact on the ground?
- How can we deliver **a more personalised experience** for donors to grow support?

Five Questions for Intermediaries (Foundations, Advisors)
- Are we really focusing on the **right big issues** for the next decade?
- What is the **most powerful role** that we can play to help set the most impactful agenda?
- How can we **better use data** to deliver more impact?
- How do we add **human understanding** into our analytical approach?
- Who should we **collaborate** with to have greater impact in the future?

Five Questions for Corporates
- Where can we use our existing capabilities and assets to **create new sources of value** for society?
- Who can we collaborate with **within and outside our sector** to have more impact?
- How can we better **share our views** about the big challenges in an effective way?
- How should we better **engage millennials** within our organisations?
- How do we increase **social and environmental capital alongside financial capital**?

Five Questions for Government
- Are we really **focusing on the most important** big issues for the next decade?
- To what extent can we better use **taxation and policy** to influence behaviours?
- How can we work better with others to help **set the most impactful** agenda?
- Are we leaving the **most appropriate gaps** in social support for philanthropy to fill?
- How should we change our approach to engage better with the **needs and interests of the next generation**?

Key Insights from Global Workshops

Each expert discussion covered a wide range of issues and then focused on some of the key topics that will have impact in the future. This is a summary of the main issues raised per location grouped into three themes:

- Challenges that are seen as important to address
- Opportunities that are already on the radar
- Future Issues that are emerging and will become more important

In addition, we have included some key statements from the events

Mumbai 21 April 2017

Challenges	1. Attracting the best talent when working in the social sector is an undesirable choice for many
2. Investing in the building of philanthropic capability when the focus is on the end impact
3. Better engaging with millennials who want to be more involved and see impact
Opportunities	1. More data enables better resources optimisation
2. Partnerships for impact where everyone contributes unique value
3. Digital engagement across the broad range of stakeholders
Future Issues	1. More organisations willing to take 'big bets' and move from serving to solving problems
2. Broader collaboration between NGOs, government and the private sector requires focus
3. Increasing state influence in directing philanthropic focus and using taxation to drive this
By 2030:	"We will have moved the needle, learned lessons and have clearer measures of success."
"Better data enables us to Give More and Give Better."
"The private sector is playing a more important role in international collaboration for development."

Singapore 25 April 2017

Challenges	1. Will a community know best what the priority issues are? More than an NGO?
2. Accommodating a changing role and purpose of business
3. Not missing out on the potential from deeper digital engagement
Opportunities	1. More funding by organisations that support beneficiary outcomes rather than personal preferences
2. Greater collaboration between charities
3. Philanthropy that is brand and business purpose driven
Future Issues	1. Community focused and community run initiatives with strong donor support
2. Co-created policies with government and greater government accountability
3. Leveraging crowd-funding without conflicting with anti money-laundering regulation
By 2030:	"Philanthropy will shift from traditional giving to impact driven capacity building."
"Proliferation of consumer and company owners who want to create and leave positive legacies."
"Need to change the China business model from focus just on money to also creating good."

Kuala Lumpur 27 April 2017

Challenges	1. Making it easier for women to get grants and microloans 2. The need for greater transparency of fund flow and impact from younger donors 3. Getting to grips with Natural Capital – as an impact measure and cost
Opportunities	1. Wider involvement of more women in key decision making 2. Co-funding between corporations that are working towards common goals 3. Shift from large companies providing funds to smaller donor populations
Future Issues	1. Authentication of activities and impact enabled by greater digital transparency 2. Greater focus on planetary boundaries and environmental impacts 3. Faith driven philanthropy drives more structured and systematic giving
By 2030:	"Greater community engagement drives better understanding of what is really needed." "More pressure from funders on NGOs to become more professional increases focus on quantitative outcomes (at the expense of qualitative ones)." "Growing wealth gap drives a growing awareness of philanthropy as a means of trying to bridge the gap."

Oxford 19 June 2017

Challenges	1. Negative reaction from broader society as focus on how original wealth is generated 2. Political campaign-funded philanthropy which may be technology driven using AI 3. Growing pressure on philanthropic organisations to use data to increase transparency
Opportunities	1. Longer-term patient capital 2. More collaboration and SPVs (special purpose vehicles) 3. Global agenda's influencing local policy
Future Issues	1. Blockchain will enable better understanding of financial and impact flows 2. Close collaboration with Government to address the impact of the increased automation of the workforce 3. Disengagement from traditional systems as more of the super-rich start their own foundations
By 2030:	"Stronger connections will be made between philanthropy and the impact it creates." "Philanthropy will become more interconnected with other sectors" "Philanthropic giving becomes expected of the 'famous billionaire'"

London (1) 28 June 2017

Challenges
1. The inevitable rise in extreme wealth amongst the few
2. More data is not necessarily better as it sometimes makes us focus on the wrong issue
3. Emotional philanthropic giving to underfunded and ineffective bodies

Opportunities
1. A lot more sharing of idea, models and efficiencies
2. In the UK the increased cultural diversity will shape philanthropic giving
3. More collaborative organisations which are non-emotional so more effective

Future Issues
1. Women will have more wealth and therefore donate more and have greater influence
2. Business and charitable sectors merge as they become increasingly pressured to appeal to millennials
3. Philanthropists get behind social movements

By 2030:
"There will be lots of surprises as increased access to data reveals what was previously unknowable."

"A move away from the complexity and systems-based thinking to a more data driven transactional approach."

"Technology allows private capital to be deployed in a way that reinforces inequality and control."

London (2) 4 July 2017

Challenges
1. Organisations pay lip service to SDGs as they are too broad to have impact
2. Diasporas often consider "home" to be their country of origin
3. Growing fragmentation of philanthropy

Opportunities
1. Reduction in international aid results in increased local philanthropy
2. Where there is a business advantage, Indian investment in philanthropy will grow
3. Divestment from morally ambiguous funds grows and focus turns to ESG investment

Future Issues
1. Money from India will be for India… and money from China is for China
2. Social media will force transparency for donors and for charities
3. As millennials become wealthier there is an increased investment in ethical matters

By 2030:
"There is an increase in philanthropic giving from Asia as global wealth shifts eastwards."

"As global turmoil increases philanthropy is forced to focus on damage limitation rather than positive change."

"Emotional philanthropy will continue to dominate but strategic philanthropy will help focus funds."

Washington DC 17 July 2017

Challenges
1. Younger generation are impatient and disruptive – they want faster impact
2. US philanthropy will be pressurized to give locally as the US government retrenches
3. Philanthropy needs to tread softly on cultural and political values

Opportunities
1. Data will change where donations flows and give confidence as the impact that is being made
2. Islamic giving has mandated $250Bn p.a.
3. Improved feedback loops between the consumer and beneficiary

Future Issues
1. People will expect to have a voice
2. How does constituent voice and politics work together?
3. Industries will move together as collectives

By 2030:
"Trust shifts to individuals and giving between individuals rather than via intermediaries or institutions."
"US and UK will no longer be the centre as wealth and power shifts toward India and China."
"There is a formalisation of the philanthropic sector's role in filling the gaps left by government."

Quito 20 July 2017

Challenges
1. Mass migration will drive a change in priorities
2. Disconnected ecosystem – a disconnect between donor and recipient
3. Isolated initiatives due to regulatory constraints

Opportunities
1. Companies more aware of their impact on local communities
2. Stronger integration between public policy and the private sector = with a broader set of measures in place
3. High impact measures are linked to real needs

Future Issues
1. South-South giving will have more legitimacy and more transparency
2. Standardised methodologies for reporting
3. Increasing state influence on scale and focus of philanthropy

By 2030:
"Increased consciousness of social responsibility in the next generation."
"Social responsibility becomes a social norm – with citizens aware of and understanding how they can contribute."
"More Partnerships between Government, companies and civil society."

58

Dubai 24 September 2017

Challenges	1. Increased importance of cross-sector working, cutting down barriers between siloes 2. A shift from treating the symptoms to providing empowerment, creating entrepreneurship and employment 3. It will remain challenging to mobilise the many, who do not see the need, to give more
Opportunities	1. Islamic finance has the possibility to create innovative products 2. Increased transparency will drive more local initiatives 3. Next generation of donors care more and will have the tools (e.g. digital, connected, global view & money) to make a difference
Future Issues	1. Increasing state influence limit opportunity in this region 2. Global initiatives attract money away from the region as Gulf philanthropists are concerned that local NGOs are unable to have impact 3. There is a greater focus on transparency and accountability
By 2030:	"The current philanthropic system will become market and demand driven, allowing full transparency and accountability." "Beneficiaries will become more engaged in the giving process so that fund allocation can better match need." "Large scale giving shifts from an elite model to one which will become more democratic so policy initiatives more accurately reflect popular sentiment."

References

i. http://www.philanthropy-impact.org/sites/default/files/downloads/bnp_paribas_philanthropy_gb.pdf
ii. www.fdnweb.org/ffdf/files/2014/.../philanthropy-in-europe-overview-2015-report.pdf
iii. https://givingusa.org/see-the-numbers-giving-usa-2017-infographic/
iv. https://www.theguardian.com/global-development/2017/sep/13/bill-gates-foundation-dont-expect-pick-up-the-bill-for-sweeping-aid-cuts-trump
v. https://avpn.asia/insights/social-investment-landscape-asia/
vi. http://ngochina.blogspot.co.uk/2017/12/font-face-font-family-timesfont-face.html
vii. http://philanthropyoutlook.com/wp-content/uploads/2016/01/Philanthropy_Outlook_2016_2017.pdf
viii. https://www.ubs.com/microsites/billionaires-report/en/new-value.html
ix. https://www.forbes.com/sites/karstenstrauss/2017/10/16/how-the-giving-habits-of-the-super-rich-are-changing/#d7ab9a834925
x. http://www.bain.com/publications/articles/india-philanthropy-report-2017.aspx
xi. https://www.cafamerica.org/trends-in-diaspora-giving-and-global-impact/
xii. https://www.theguardian.com/global-development-professionals-network/2016/nov/29/community-philanthropy-a-brave-new-model-for-development-funding
xiii. https://www2.deloitte.com/global/en/pages/about-deloitte/articles/millennialsurvey.html#
xiv. http://www3.weforum.org/docs/WEF_II_FromMarginsMainstream_Report_2013.pdf
xv. http://www.newsweek.com/red-cross-harvey-relief-numbers-troubling-trend-657542   http://www.express.co.uk/news/uk/758803/Oxfam-scandal-sex-abuse-corruption-deaths
xvi. quote from Laura Arrillaga- Andreessen, lecturer at Stanford University Graduate School of Business
xvii. http://thinkcity.com.my/
xviii. http://www.npr.org/, www.bbc.co.uk
xix. http://www.royalfoundation.com/heads-together-duke-duchess-cambridge-prince-harry-working-eliminate-stigma-around-mental-health/
xx. https://thediplomat.com/2017/06/the-wechat-phenomenon-social-media-with-chinese-characteristics/
xxi. https://www.inbreakthrough.tv,

https://en.wikipedia.org/wiki/Balika_Vadhu , http://www.livemint.com/Consumer/Nu6BTh8c6lc6UQcThQv4ZI/Why-wait-for-a-tragedy-to-happen-asks-Tata-Tea-in-its-new-.html
xxii. https://en.wikipedia.org/wiki/Giving_circle
xxiii. https://nonprofitquarterly.org/2017/03/15/crowdfunding-will-change-philanthropy/
xxiv. http://tpw.org/events/entry/the_philanthropy_workshops_perspectives_on_philanthropists_special_report
xxv. https://www.economist.com/news/finance-and-economics/21719494-rise-dafs-may-be-much-about-tax-charity-philanthropic-boom
xxvi. https://www.kickstarter.com/, https://www.seedrs.com/, https://www.justgiving.com/,https://gofundme.com
xxvii. http://www.cancerresearchuk.org/support-us/citizen-science
xxviii. https://en.wikipedia.org/wiki/Slacktivism
xxix. https://en.wikipedia.org/wiki/Harambee
xxx. https://www.givedirectly.org/efficiency
xxxi. http://www.kiva.org/about
xxxii. https://www.princeton.edu/~joha/publications/Haushofer_Shapiro_UCT_2016.04.25.pdf
xxxiii. www.oxfam.org.uk/donate/content/iraq-a1

Contact Details

The programme and report were conducted and written by the following members of the Future Agenda team:

Dr Tim Jones, co-Founder –
tim.jones@futureagenda.org
https://www.linkedin.com/in/innovationstrategy/

Caroline Dewing, co-Founder –
caroline.dewing@futureagenda.org
https://www.linkedin.com/in/caroline-dewing-0077051/

James Alexander, Director –
james.alexander@futureagenda.org
https://www.linkedin.com/in/james-alexander-617747/

www.ingramcontent.com/pod-product-compliance
Lightning Source LLC
Chambersburg PA
CBHW051919210526
45473CB00006B/2071